# From a
# BAKER'S
# KITCHEN

D1737501

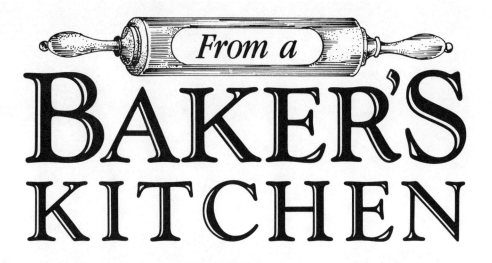

# From a
# BAKER'S
# KITCHEN

## Techniques and Recipes for Professional Quality Baking in the Home Kitchen

*by*

## Gail Sher

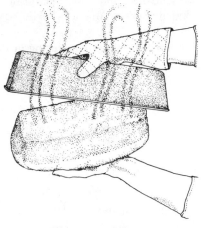

*illustrated by*

## Mimi Osborne

**ARIS BOOKS**
**Addison-Wesley Publishing Company, Inc.**
Reading, Massachusetts   Menlo Park, California   New York
Don Mills, Ontario   Wokingham, England   Amsterdam   Bonn
Sydney   Singapore   Tokyo   Madrid   San Juan

Copyright © 1984 by Gail Sher
Illustrations © 1984 by Mimi Osborne

"Country Fair Egg Bread" by Dolores Casella, from *A World of Breads*, published by David White, Inc., One Pleasant Ave., Port Washington, NY 11050. © 1966.

All rights reserved. No part of this publication may be reproduced, stored in a retrieval system, or transmitted, in any form or by any means, electronic, mechanical, photocopying, recording, or otherwise, without the prior written permission of the publisher. Printed in the United States of America. Published simultaneously in Canada.

**Library of Congress Cataloging-in-Publication Data**

Sher, Gail, 1942–
    From a baker's kitchen.

    Bibliography: p.
    Includes index.
    1. Baking.        I. Title.
TX763.S427    1988        641.8′15        88-35062
ISBN 0-201-11539-5

(Previously published by Harris Publishing Co.,
ISBN 0-943186-11-0, pbk.)

Composition by Ann Flanagan
Typography in Goudy Oldstyle
Cover and book design by Fifth Street Design

Aris Books Editorial Office
and Test Kitchen
1621 Fifth St.
Berkeley, CA 94710

ABCDEFGHIJ-VB-898
First Addison-Wesley printing, December 1988

# CONTENTS

# RECIPE INDEX

## YEASTED BREADS

# QUICK BREADS

# Acknowledgements

This book would not have been possible without the hovering care of my friend Merry White Benezra. Her repeated readings of the manuscript and constant unearthings of often humorous ambiguities contributed enormously to what I hope is now a clear and precise text. I am likewise indebted to Beau Beausoleil for entitling the book, to Maureen Reynolds and Barbara Horn for meticulous (beyond the call of duty) testing of the recipes and to Peter Overton and Steve Sullivan for professional criticism.

In addition, I would like to thank Marjorie Rice, Sahag Avedisian, and Sherry Virbila for reading the manuscript and offering their suggestions; and to thank the enthusiastic staff at Aris for support and use of their recipe testing kitchen.

# Introduction

I have always thought that it lies specifically within the realm of the home baker to bake the very best bread, the bread that matches his own ideals perfectly. By perfectly, I mean in such a way as to allow carefully selected ingredients to come to their peak of taste. Except for the special ovens and steam-producing equipment required by breads such as French bread, the home baker is in a better position than the professional to make perfect loaves. A baker with a business must always be considering the cost of ingredients, the overall schedule of everything made in his shop, the availability of supplies in large quantities, procedures that must work simultaneously with many other procedures, normal business hours, efficiency in terms of employee times, overhead, and on and on. Having only yourself or your family to consider, your loaves can be tailor-made to suit your exact taste without preservatives, without adulterated ingredients (powdered eggs, for instance), and offering, with a little know-how, a fuller, more intense flavor.

In writing about baking, I must explain that I consider myself to be a disciple of Elizabeth David. *English Bread & Yeast Cookery* (1980) is a staggering accomplishment. Nevertheless, I know that many people have not read this book with the care that it deserves and that some find it difficult to use as a recipe book. There seems to be a need for a bread book that maintains Elizabeth David's level of integrity yet is straightforward and easy to grasp. Thus I have designed *From a Baker's Kitchen* to be, to use a baking metaphor, elastic. You can read it and apply it immediately but, as your knowledge and understanding expand, you will be able to assimilate the information more and more fully. The text will grow as you grow and may be read on several levels.

*From a Baker's Kitchen* is divided into five parts. Part I concerns ingredients. Although proper rising, kneading and oven techniques are important, these procedures are only going to be as effective as the ingredients on which they work. *You* are *eating* these ingredients. Their quality and freshness will make a difference not only to the taste of your bread, but also to its nutritional value. In time your familiarity with the ingredients of bread making will lead you to a style that is your own.

Part I begins with a chapter on grains. Definitions of commonly available flours are provided, along with a short dictionary of the more exotic specialty flours with which I encourage you to experiment. Every flour that will appear later in a recipe is defined and explained.

There follows a chapter on leaveners in which natural leaveners, aerating leaveners, chemical leaveners, and yeast are contrasted; a short chapter describing the function of salt in bread making; a chapter on liquids, shortening and eggs; and, finally, a chapter on embellishments, the use of which, though easy, must be clearly understood.

Part II is called *Methods and Principles of Bread Making*. Now that you know about what you are putting into your bread, you need to know how to do it; that is, you need to know about the *process*. *The idea of process is the key to this book*. Given identical ingredients, two bakers using different methods would attain entirely different results. This is because certain chemical changes must occur in the ingredients in order for bread to be bread. Your job as baker is simply to provide the environment in which these changes can most easily occur. The more you know about what you are doing, the less physical labor you will have to exert. The dough itself happily does almost everything if it is just allowed to. In bread making, correct methods and principles boil down to your learning how to allow your dough to ripen on its own. Thus you can bake bread using time-consuming processes, but it need not be *your* time. For the most part you do not even have to supervise.

Part III is called *Guidelines for Equipment*. I have found that there is some confusion about many kitchen utensils essential for making bread and quick breads. The equipment is listed and described in the order in which it would be used in the sponge method of bread making. At the end there is a section on cleaning up after baking. Everyone who bakes eventually has to clean up and, true to form, even here, dough has its own very particular demands.

In Part IV is an explanation of the sponge method technique, which is not at all a new technique. In the beginning of *Jude the Obscure*, Hardy describes Jude setting his sponge in the evening, kneading and baking his bread early the following morning and studying Latin while making his deliveries in the bright light of day. What *is* new is the idea that one can easily adapt this method to a busy modern life. There is a general misconception that bread takes too much time to make at home, especially if one must use old-fashioned, long-rise methods. Lately, these have been supplanted by much-touted short-rise techniques. This is a pity. My purpose is to show how a long-rise method is not only superior in terms of the ultimate flavor of the bread but also can be even *more* accommodating to a busy schedule in that the dough may be worked upon at intervals, and the bread will enormously benefit. The sponge method may be divided into five steps and it is here that I explain each of them fully. I have included, by way of a sample, a typical bread recipe and explained step by step how to convert it to the sponge method. For those who are skeptical of the sponge method's superiority, I might suggest that you begin with your own favorite bread, translate it, and see for yourself the vast difference this wonderful technique makes.

Part V of the book consists of recipes. About one-fourth of the recipes are for yeast-raised breads, which are presented with roman numbers to indicate the five steps of the sponge method. You are encouraged to refer back to the special section on the sponge method (Part IV) to refresh your memory on each step until these procedures become automatic. (It would have been too cumbersome to include the details of each step of the sponge method with every recipe.*) I further propose that the beginning baker choose one of the breads (perhaps an unadorned whole-wheat bread) and make it a number of times until the sponge method itself is more or less routine. Any variations or problems that crop up will then be identifiable as differences in technique and can be dealt with right away before matters become complicated by a variety of ingredients, any one of which could also be culpable. The first step is to learn *how* to use the sponge method. Then you will be able to make the best version of any bread imaginable.

There are also recipes for various kinds of quick breads. I

---

*Although we have made it as easy as possible for the home baker to flip back and forth between the yeast-raised bread recipes and the section on the sponge method by coloring the edges of the pages of Part IV, you can get a separate Sponge Method section in the form of a booklet from the publisher by sending a $1.50 check or money order payable to Aris Books, 1621 Fifth St., Berkeley, CA 94710.

include them to encourage you to make authentic *quick* breads when you want to save time rather than try to condense or manipulate the recipe for a long-rising bread, which will only be to its detriment and your disappointment. Corn breads, spoonbreads, muffins, and the like are deeply entrenched in our baking heritage and are at their best when mixed quickly and served straight from the oven.

Lastly, there is (like cleaning after baking) the neglected but ever-present problem of what to do with bread that is leftover. There is *much* to be done with stale bread. No crumb of your well-selected ingredients carefully baked into loaves need ever be thrown away. After enjoying it in its original form, you may turn bread into melba toast, croutons, elegant breakfast casseroles, soups, poultry stuffing, or puddings. This chapter was difficult to contain. The recipes chosen will provide enjoyable meals and ideas on which to improvise many more.

# BREAD INGREDIENTS

# GRAINS

**What is a grain?**

Grains are the seeds or fruit of a cereal grass. Ground very fine, such seeds become flour, which is the main ingredient in bread. Flour for bread is most often milled from all or part of the wheat berry, but many other grains and even vegetables can be made into suitable flours. A cross section of these various seeds shows them to be similarly composed of three basic parts:

**Bran** Bran is the shell of the seed, consisting of several layers of cellulose. Even when ground, it is not considered a flour but a fiber, which is indigestible and will not react with yeast. Fiber, however, is sometimes a desirable ingredient in bread. Bran has a mild earthy taste and adds a coarse, flaky texture to bread.

**Germ** At the base of the grain near the stem is the germ or embryo of the future plant. It contains oil, protein, iron, and vitamins B and E. Because the germ will easily turn rancid, it is removed in commercial milling, whereby its delicious nut taste is also lost.

**Endosperm** The bulk of the grain is the endosperm, which nourishes the germ. Though mostly starch, it also has gluten-producing proteins and minerals such as phosphorous, magnesium, iron, zinc, copper, and manganese. This part of the grain, tasting subtly sweet, is that from which ordinary white flour is milled.

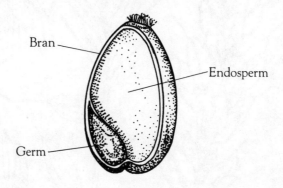

Bran

Endosperm

Germ

**What is gluten?**

Though flour milled from any grain (or vegetable or bean or nut) can be used to make bread, *for bread that will rise* one needs a flour that contains a protein called gluten. Actually there are two protein elements, glutenin and gliadin, that are distinct from each other in the dry state. With a liquid as a catalyst, the gluten molecules link together and form a sheath of little bubbles that trap the carbon dioxide released by the growing yeast. They also hold the other ingredients in suspension. As the yeast expands further, the filaments of gluten stretch to contain the new yeast cells and their gaseous by-products. Eventually it is the meshing of these gas pockets that constitutes the final texture of the bread. Thus, the more gluten a flour contains, the greater is going to be its capacity to form a tenacious mass of dough that will rise evenly. Bread is able to maintain its shape after the yeast dies because the now developed and set gluten holds it up. If a network of gluten were not formed, the gas would just escape and the bread would lose its desirable porous quality.

**Where is the gluten found?**

Gluten is primarily found in wheat berries. Wheat flours are favored for leavened breads because only wheat has enough gluten to achieve the desirable lightness. This means white flour, whole-wheat flour, and gluten flour. Rye and triticale flours have gluten but not enough to raise loaves very high. Other cereal flours contains only traces of gluten; those milled from nuts, vegetables, or beans have none at all.

# White Flours

**Bread flour**

For baking, wheat falls into two main categories of suitability. The first category is associated with the season in which the wheat is planted. Spring wheat, planted in spring and harvested in autumn, produces a strong (hard) flour containing high percentages of gluten (between twelve and fifteen percent). Winter wheat, planted in autumn and harvested in early summer, has less gluten (between ten and twelve percent). Because it stays in the ground longer, winter wheat is usually tastier than spring wheat. Spring wheat will absorb more water and must be kneaded longer, but yields bread with a stronger structure and greater volume; winter wheat yields a fuller-flavored loaf.

The second category is characterized simply by whether the wheat is of the type known as *hard* or *soft*. Hard wheat (which may be either winter or spring wheat) has kernels that are hard and difficult to cut. Its relatively high percentage of gluten makes it tough and resistant, very well suited to bread. The kernels of soft wheat are soft and appear starchy when cut. Its small percentage of gluten makes the flour weak and not good for bread though very suitable for biscuits, muffins, and pastries.

**All-purpose flour**

All-purpose flour is a mixture of hard and soft wheats with a gluten content of approximately eight percent. Though quick breads and muffins do quite well when made from all-purpose flour, it is not ideal for either yeast-raised breads or pastries. The fact that it is now ubiquitous has, unfortunately, made both hard and soft wheat flours difficult to obtain.

**Cake flour**

Cake flour is made from soft spring wheat. It has more starch and even less gluten than all-purpose flour and is used for pastries in which a delicate and flaky texture is desired.

**New Bread Flour**

Since 1982, a new mixture of flours labeled *Bread Flour* has become available. It is a combination of high gluten flour and barley malt flour, to which potassium bromate, a dough conditioner, has been added. This new product causes the dough to rise overly fast so that the true texture and flavor of the wheat do not have sufficient opportunity to develop. Therefore it is not recommended.

**Bleached versus unbleached flour**

As flour ages, it naturally whitens. Since the purpose of bleaching is to create the whitest possible flour, bleaching can also be understood as a method of instant aging. Aged white flour performs better in machine-made dough. Thus its current popularity is easy to understand: most commercial bakeries employ machines for their bulk production. Bleaching chemicals, however, destroy the vitamin B and the fresh taste apparent in unbleached flour.

# Milling

**Commercial milling**

Milling is the process by which whole grains become flour. Most commercially available flours are milled by gigantic high-speed rollers that revolve at between six hundred fifty and eight hundred revolutions a minute. Because such speed generates enough heat to destroy the vitamins and oxidize the oil in the germ, the latter is removed before rolling begins. Since the germ is the most nutritious part of the grain, nutrients must be added later to commercially milled flour.

**Stone grinding**

Grains pulverized between stone grinding wheels or buhr-stones (sometimes turned by water wheels) working at about two hundred revolutions a minute, are referred to as stone-ground or, occasionally, water-ground grains. Since the friction of the stones generates only a small amount of heat, the composition of the grain is barely changed. Alice Waters says that, "unless the whole-grain flours. . . are stone-ground and absolutely fresh, they will contribute nothing more than their color to the bread."[1]

**Home grinding**

A wheat spikelet

The freshest, most nutritious flour is made by grinding whole wheat berries in your own kitchen. Home grinders, however, are expensive and the flour that you mill will contain large flakes of bran. Because these particles of bran inhibit aeration, whole-wheat flour is not *always* what you will want for your bread. On the other hand, if you prefer a light textured bread, you will have the further task of sifting out the coarsest part of the bran. If you enjoy the density and texture that the bran flakes contribute, a home grinder assures you absolutely of having it.

Be selective. Most electric grinders for home use run hot, thereby, as in commercial milling, destroying the dormant life of the germ. Hand mills are more certain to keep the grain's nutritional value intact.

If you can find a source, it is worth buying freshly milled stone-ground flour in small quantities. This type of flour will already have the bran ground to a medium-fine texture.

**Food processed grains**

For those with food processors there is another alternative.[2] Soften whole grains by covering them with hot water and allowing them to soak overnight or, cover them with boiling water and allow them to soak for three hours. Drain, mix with a small amount of flour, and process in a food processor, using the metal blade, for approximately two minutes. This method gives one all the benefits of a whole grain—the protein, vitamins, minerals, oil and fiber (bran) content —in what could be, if one wishes, a very light textured bread. You can also use a coffee mill to grind unsoaked grain.

# Whole-Wheat Flours and Meals

**Whole-wheat flour**
Whole-wheat flour is ground from the whole wheat berry. Thus it includes the outer layers of bran, high in non-nutritive fiber, the germ, rich in oil, protein, iron and vitamins, and the endosperm, which is primarily starch but also contains the gluten-producing proteins and many minerals. The flavor of the bran and germ will emerge and blend with the flavor of the other ingredients noticeably better when doughs containing them are allowed to rise for a long time. Because the oils in the germ turn rancid when exposed to air, whole meals and flours must be used immediately or stored in cool, airtight containers.

**Whole-wheat meal**
Whole-wheat meal is ground coarsely from the whole kernel of wheat and the rough bits of bran are left in.

**Whole-wheat pastry flour**
Whole-wheat pastry flour is also ground from the whole wheat kernel, but it is finely milled so that its texture is light, making it perfect for pies, biscuits, and pastries.

**Graham flour**
Graham flour bears the name of Sylvester Graham, a nineteenth-century crusader against commercial white bread. Like whole-wheat flour, it is produced by grinding the whole wheat berry, but in this case the bran is not ground to a finer consistency. The term is often loosely applied to coarsely ground whole-wheat flour.

**Cracked wheat**
Cracked wheat (bulgur) is cut, instead of ground, from the whole wheat berry and adds a wonderful crunchy texture and nutty flavor to bread.

**Specialty flours**
Because of their high gluten content, wheat flours are the most widely used for bread. Many other foods can be ground into flours with which, in combination with wheat, it is possible to make highly nutritious, light-textured breads. Since there is some confusion about the nature of these flours, what follows is a short dictionary of specialty flours and related meals and grains.

**Gluten flour**
Gluten flour is made by washing the starch from the endosperm of the wheat berry. High in protein and low in starch, it is used for special diets and as an additive to yeasted doughs made with flours containing small amounts of gluten. Since a limited amount of gluten will give a dough a limited

capacity to rise, a lighter loaf will result if about five or ten percent of a low-gluten flour is replaced with pure gluten flour.

**Semolina flour**

Semolina flour is milled from hard durum wheat. After the bran is removed from the wheat berry and before what remains is ground into flour, the largest particles of the endosperm may be detached. These are known as semolina. It is thought to make the finest textured wheat flour and is usually used for making pasta. With its rich creamy flavor and consistency, semolina bread has been lovingly nicknamed "ice-cream bread."

**Rye flours**

After wheat, rye flour milled from the whole rye grain is the flour most suitable for bread. To compensate for its gluten deficiency, you can add it to a pre-raised base of white or whole-wheat flour. While the glutenous wheat strengthens and stabilizes the rye's more fragile gluten structure, the rye adds a distinct flavor and smoothness to the bread. Large amounts of this heavy flour will weigh a dough down, making it sticky and slow to rise. This is true for all grades of rye and progressively more true the darker the grade. If necessary you can compensate for this to some extent by raising rye doughs in warmer places.

Rye flour comes in four different grades distinguished by the quantities of bran. White rye is a light, rather delicately colored and flavored flour. The bran is removed when the whole rye grain is ground. Medium rye is a blend of dark and white rye flours. It has a full, slightly sour taste. The bran is often not included when medium rye is milled. Dark rye always contains the bran. It has a full and very pronounced sour taste. Though often confused with dark rye, pumpernickel flour is distinguished by an even higher proportion of bran.

Rye breads, often an amalgam of many different kinds of ingredients, are best served the day after baking. This allows the various flavors to mellow, and being slightly stale, the loaves are easier to slice thinly as suits their richness. Because of their density, rye breads retain moisture well and, if stored properly (see page 66), will stay fresh quite a bit longer than lighter breads.

**Triticale**

Triticale (pronounced trit-i-kay-lee) is a man-made hybrid, a cross between wheat and rye. Its berries have three or four percent more, higher quality protein (the essential amino acids being better balanced) than other grains. Though the taste of triticale is associated with rye, it has a distinctive light sweetness. Like rye, however, its gluten is somewhat fragile and triticale does best when blended with high-gluten wheat flour. A workable proportion is one-third triticale to two-thirds wheat, but you can use more, depending on your tolerance for a heavy texture.

**Corn flour**

Rich in oils and vitamins, corn produces a cream-colored flour with a naturally sweet flavor. It has no gluten but may be combined in small quantities with a high-gluten flour to make yeasted breads. Cornstarch does not have enough body to be used in bread. It is used, rather, as a sauce thickener.

**Cornmeal**

Cornmeal is coarsely ground dried corn. It may be white or yellow but it must be *whole*, containing the nutritious germ missing in supermarket varieties. Look for stone-ground or water-ground cornmeal. It will add a crunchy texture and sweet taste to your bread.

**Hominy and grits**

Hominy is corn that has been hulled and dried; coarsely ground hominy is called *grits*.

**Rolled oats**

Rolled oats are whole oat kernels compressed into flakes by heavy steel rollers. They add a meaty chewiness to bread.

**Oat flour**

Though its gluten is very poor, oat flour is rich in minerals, fat, and a natural antioxidant (which acts as a preservative), making it a welcome addition to bread. Ground from oat groats by a painstaking process, its mild, sweet, earthy flavor justifies the considerable trouble necessary to obtain it.

**Potato flour**

The potato is a tuber, not a grain, though its starch is the same as that of grains. The nutritional value and smooth, rich, sweet flavor offset its relatively high milling costs. Potato flour will not absorb liquids as readily as wheat flour will, but it activates fermentation and is easy to knead. Breads with even a small amount of potato flour will rise faster, bake faster, and keep very well. Even the addition of potato water (the water in which potatoes have been cooked) will prolong the life of bread.

**Buckwheat flour**

Buckwheat is not a grain and therefore not a relative of wheat. Indeed it is a member of the rhubarb family. Ground from groats, buckwheat flour is heavy but highly nourishing and has a marvelous flavor (enhanced by roasting) unlike any other flour. It is hearty and particularly well suited to cold climates.

**Barley flour**    Barley flour is milled from the whole kernel of barley. It is moist and mildly sweet and adds a cakelike texture to bread. The flavor of barley flour is also enhanced by roasting.

**Whole millet**    Millet is one of the oldest known grains. Because of its bland taste (nutlike and slightly sweet), superb texture, and richness (it is high in protein), it blends exceptionally well with a wide variety of ingredients (flours, meals, dried fruits, and cheeses), mellowing them yet supplying an unexpected crunchiness.

**Storing flour**    Ideally, flour should be used immediately and not stored at all. If you must store it, however, the best place is the freezer and, next best, a dry, well-ventilated storeroom. Since flour absorbs moisture and odors, a damp place near foods such as cheese, onions, or coffee would not be suitable.

# LEAVENERS

**What is leavening?**

The word *leaven* is derived from the Latin word *levare* meaning "to raise." A leavener added to batters or doughs will result, not merely in more volume, but also in a more distinctive cellular structure, a more developed flavor, and a more integrated texture than would result if the same ingredients were baked without one.

**Natural leaveners**

Heat alone is enough to raise light batters and soft, flat doughs such as that used for chappatis. Moisture, in the presence of heat, turns to steam, which puffs up the dough. Even more dramatic puffing will result if beaten eggs (an aerating leavener) are used. In popovers, for example, as the batter's liquid turns to steam in the heat of the oven, the proteins in the flour and beaten eggs enmesh forming an elastic shell that traps the steam inside. The air and liquid trapped inside continue heating and swelling until the temperature is reached at which the protein coagulates and the expanded structure solidifies. Heat and steam are natural leaveners and are used either alone or with the three other basic leaveners: aerating leaveners (e.g., eggs), chemical leaveners, and yeast.

**Yeast**

Yeast is the oldest leavener. It is a living, one-celled fungus that, in the presence of flour and water, feeds, grows, and reproduces new cells. During this process, it turns oxygen and simple sugars into carbon dioxide and alcohol. The carbon dioxide becomes trapped in the glutenous fibers of the dough causing it to expand or rise. The small amount of alcohol produced by the yeast evaporates during baking.

**Kinds of yeast**

There are many varieties of yeast including wild spores floating at any given time in the air. These ferment wine, beer, vinegar, and "sourdough," which was the first kind of leavened bread. There is also brewers' yeast, which is a nutritional supplement yeast, and bakers' yeast which is classified as *Saccharomyces cerevisiae*. Within this species are various strains.

## Compressed yeast

Compressed yeast was the earliest yeast manufactured for baking. It consists of microscopic yeast cells compressed into a solid block. One ounce of compressed yeast contains several billion cells. Since it is still active, it is highly perishable. Even under refrigeration, it will keep only for about ten days to two weeks. It may be frozen for as long as two months. After this it will turn moldy and deteriorate. Compressed yeast is sold in half-ounce cakes, which should be dissolved in 80°F liquid before being added to dough.

## Active dry yeast

Active dry yeast was developed during World War II. Dried yeasts are in spore form, a condition in which the cells are temporarily inactive but can still become activated when more favorable conditions are provided. Active dry yeast requires no special handling and, if kept refrigerated, will remain active for months. After rehydration, it is used exactly like compressed yeast. Both are equally nutritious, consisting of, approximately, fourteen or fifteen percent protein, seventy percent moisture, ten to twelve percent carbohydrates, and between two and three percent minerals, enzymes, and vitamins, the latter primarily of the B complex group. The enzymes cause the fermentation, releasing the carbon dioxide that leavens the bread.

Fleischmann's Red Star yeast is readily available in one-quarter-ounce packets (the usual quantity needed for up to three loaves of bread) and need not be refrigerated or proofed provided it is used before the date stamped on the envelope. To proof yeast, dissolve the amount called for in the recipe in one-quarter of a cup of lukewarm liquid before adding the rest of the ingredients. If it bubbles within five or ten minutes, you have proof that it is alive.

## Instant dried yeast

Recently a different strain of yeast commercially known as *instant dried yeast* has been developed. This yeast has been dried to a lower percentage of moisture than active dry yeast. It has been combined with an emulsifier and a form of sugar that immediately activates it in the presence of a warm liquid. The drying process also leaves three times as many alive yeast cells as are to be found in active dried yeast. Instant dried yeast has a 9 to 12 month shelf-life. Because it is so active, quantities may be reduced by a third, and because it is so reliable, proofing is not necessary. Its results have been acceptable for all doughs except those that require either a lot of sugar (for which it has a low tolerance) or a slow rising at low temperatures. Some bakers do not like the taste that this strain of yeast produces.

*Note:* The protein content of instant dried yeast also has a flavor that some bakers find disagreeable.

**Red Star Quick Rise Yeast**

Red Star Quick Rise Yeast, a new strain of highly active yeast developed by Universal Foods Corporation in 1982, allows dough to rise up to fifty percent faster than those made with traditional yeasts. Its claims to be half as fast again are true. For bread however, there remains the question of whether or not a faster rise is desirable (see Fermentation, below, and Ripeness, page 44).

**Mixing in the yeast initially**

In contact with moisture and warmth, yeast cells divide and multiply rapidly. They remain dormant below 50°F and die at temperatures above 120°F. Thus, when first awakening the yeast with lukewarm liquid, remember that between 80°F and 100°F is the ideal temperature for compressed yeast; between 100°F and 110°F for active dry yeast. Salt inhibits the activity of yeast. Fat will coat it and slacken its growth, as will too much sugar. Thus salt, fat, or an excessive quantity of sugar should not be added until the yeast has had a chance to come to its full potency.

**Fermentation**

Fermentation (or ripening) is the chemical action that takes place when the enzymes in the yeast break down the starch in the flour, first to compound sugars, then to simple sugars, and finally to carbon dioxide gas and alcohol. Such ripening gives rise to acidity in dough and, since it is this acidity that creates the bread flavor of bread, it is primarily time or a long fermentation period that the home baker is after. Short-rise methods of breadmaking, even those of the greatest sophistication, cannot duplicate the wonderful subtle sweetness characteristic of naturally risen dough.

The longer dough is allowed to grow, moreover, the finer is going to be its texture. Using *less* yeast (thus slowing the process), rising the dough in *cooler* places, kneading well, punching down, and allowing the stretching process to repeat itself—all contribute to a full flavor and a beautifully even crumb.

In doubling a recipe, one does not increase the yeast in increments commensurate with other ingredients. As a rule of thumb, use one teaspoon of active dry yeast for every loaf of bread. If you are allowing long risings, half a teaspoon to a loaf will suffice.

**What happens to yeast in the oven?**

In the oven, yeast cells grow more and more active until they finally reach a temperature that kills them. The cells nearest to the surfaces of the bread die first while those on the inside continue to reproduce and expand outwards until they, too, reach the maximum temperature. This is why there is such a difference between the cellular make-up of the inside of a loaf of bread and the crust. At 165°F, the gluten in the dough will coagulate. Continued baking dries out and solidifies this new structure.

*Note:* A loaf with a heady, yeasty taste is more likely to have been underbaked than to have had too much yeast. Underbaked bread will be moist and dense in the center and taste strongly of yeast. Test your loaves for doneness (see page 64) before removing them from the oven.

**Aerating leaveners**

Aerating leaveners work on the principle that a volatile substance will produce a vapor or gas that, when heated, expands and creates a structure that can be solidified. Examples are whipped whole eggs or egg whites, butter, and the various kinds of fats used to make baked goods. Usually air is incorporated into a batter when eggs are beaten, often separately, because egg whites will accommodate much more air than will the yolks or even the whole eggs. During baking the air increases further and the expansion will continue until the temperature is reached at which the proteins in the eggs coagulate and the newly swelled structure is fixed in place. Butter and fats are used as moisture-proof barriers that trap water vapor released during baking by alternate levels of dough and butter. The result is an aerated pastry of multiple, paper-thin layers.

**Chemical leaveners**

There are times when a baker wants more leavening action than either a natural leavener or an aerating leavener will give, and yet for various reasons perfers not to use yeast. For example, unyeasted doughs require little or no kneading. They work with the support of moisture and heat. Since their rising power does not rely on the expandability of a well-developed glutenous network, they provide an opportunity for incorporating the many delicious grains that have minimal gluten-forming potential. A baker might then select a chemical leavener (e.g., baking soda or baking powder) that, although working on a different principle, mimics the carbon-dioxide-producing activity of yeast.

**Three phases of chemical action**

In the baking process, there are three stages—mixing, rising, and baking—during which a chemical reaction can take place. The value of a chemical leavener depends on the rate at which it releases carbon dioxide during these three stages. The initial reaction (the first release of carbon dioxide) takes place during the mixing stage, through the catalyst of moisture. The release continues during the rising stage. This is the interval, after the batter is mixed and before it goes into the oven, during which rising is referred to as *bench action*—a baker's table is known as a bench. The oven's heat promotes a further, even more dramatic, release. The results often seem magical.

**Baking soda**

The important chemical reaction occurs when an alkali is mixed with an acid. One alkali commonly used is bicarbonate of soda (baking soda). To be activated, baking soda must first be neutralized by an acid which, in a recipe, appears in the form of another ingredient—citrus juice, acid fruits, molasses, honey, buttermilk, and sour cream. The leavening action requires the presence of both the alkali and the acid, so blanket substitutions in recipes using baking soda are not always possible. White sugar is not acidic, brown sugar (which contains molasses) is; molasses is, but corn syrup is not; water cannot be used in place of orange or lemon juice or vinegar; and sweet milk cannot replace buttermilk or yogurt. Apricots, raisins, bananas, and apples are less obvious acid additions. If you must omit the acid called for in a recipe, use baking powder instead (four teaspoons for every one teaspoon of baking soda) lest the batter or dough fail to rise. Conversely, if you add a second acid to a baking powder recipe (such as cranberries to plain muffins), you will need to add a small amount of baking soda to neutralize it.

**Single-acting baking powder**

The results of using baking soda in such combinations are frequently inconsistent due to the many variables involved. Baking powder, introduced in the 1850s, makes results more predictable. Single-acting baking powder (also known as phosphate baking powder) is bicarbonate of soda in combination with an acid, usually cream of tartar. When moistened, the two chemicals instantly begin to act on each other. Baking powder therefore also contains cornstarch to keep it dry so that it will not become active while in storage. The disadvantage of single-acting baking powder is that the chemical reaction, and thus the leavening, begins *immediately* after the liquid is added. If the baker is not a wizard, much of the leavening power will be lost before the batter reaches the oven.

**Double-acting baking powder**

Double-acting baking powder also begins to work immediately, but the reaction is twofold and slower. Double-acting baking powder releases gas initially during the mixing stage, but it is a gradual release. The main reaction occurs at temperatures above 140°F, that is, after the dough or batter is in the oven. Thus batters and doughs can be made ahead of time, dispensing with bench-to-oven acrobatics. The period of grace after the batter is mixed and before the baking powder begins to lose its leavening ability is between fifteen and thirty minutes.

*Note:* Most (but not all) brands of double-acting baking powder are treated with aluminum sulphate. If you prefer to avoid this chemical (undoubtedly the source of the chemical taste often associated with baking powder recipes), seek out the brands to which it is not added or make your own single-acting baking powder. (Commercial single-acting baking powder is still available but is increasingly difficult to find.) Two teaspoons of homemade single-acting baking powder will produce the same rise as one teaspoon of commercial double-acting.

For 1 teaspoon single-acting baking powder, combine:
½ teaspoon fresh cream of tartar
¼ teaspoon fresh sodium bicarbonate
¼ teaspoon arrowroot or cornstarch (optional stabilizer)

Do not attempt to store homemade baking powder. It will absorb moisture from the air and quickly lose its effectiveness.

**How much to use**

Double-acting baking powder is generally used in the ratio of one and a half teaspoons to each cup of flour. As with baking soda, too much can create a bitter taste. Theoretically, the proportions of baking powder to other dry ingredients should remain the same when a recipe is correctly multiplied and pan sizes stay the same. The variable in most brands of double-acting baking powder is the aluminum sulphate. Therefore, when doubling or tripling a recipe, use only three-quarters as much again of the baking powder. The reduced quantity will still provide enough leavening and is an alternative to having to deal with single-acting baking powder. The bicarbonate of soda that baking powder contains also destroys vitamin $B_1$. One wants to use as little as possible.

**Work quietly, gently, and quickly**

When using chemically leavened mixtures, it is important that one handle the dough gently to avoid dissipating the carbon dioxide. Working quickly prevents overhandling which, because it develops the gluten and therefore toughens the dough, must be avoided at all costs. Some baking powder recipes actually include a small amount of lemon juice or vinegar. The acid softens the gluten, improving the dough's flakiness. Resting the dough tenderizes it by relaxing any gluten present.

**Self-rising flour**

Self-rising flour is simply a commercial combination of all-purpose flour, baking powder, and salt. Bewilderingly, it is often not feasible to substitute self-rising flour for all-purpose flour even if you leave out the recipe's baking powder and salt. One explanation might be that the perfect balance of leaveners is extremely delicate—slightly but importantly different for each set of ingredients.

**Term of potency**

All chemical leavening agents, and the flours or mixes that include them, eventually lose their potency. They should be used within several months of purchase and kept air-tight in a dry place in the meantime. If there is a question about potency, stir one teaspoon into one-third of a cup of hot water. It will bubble *quickly* if it is still good.

# SALT

**Salt inhibits yeast**

Though bread without salt lacks a certain verve, it is primarily in the context of its action on the yeast that salt is important. Salt inhibits the fermentation of yeast. At the same time it strengthens the gluten and prevents the dough from becoming too sticky.

Cognizant of salt's importance, you may, within reason, vary the amount according to the length of rising time you would like to give your bread. Since salt retards the fermentation process, one can increase the quantity, which will allow the dough to rise more gradually and develop a fuller flavor. Using less will hamper the yeast less: Fermentation will be faster, rising will be faster, and the ultimate flavor of the bread will be noticeably inferior.

*Note:* The usual proportion of salt to flour is one teaspoon of salt for every two cups of flour.

**When should salt be added?**

If you add salt right away, it will constrain the yeast right away, possibly delaying its maturity. If you wait, the yeast will be able to come to its full potency before the ripening process is inhibited.

**Will it taste salty?**

The final salt flavor will be affected, not only by the quantity of salt, but also by the kind and volume of dough, since various combinations enhance or detract from a salt taste. Salt, like yeast and double-acting baking powder, is not increased proportionately with other ingredients when a recipe is multiplied. If you double a recipe, for example, you might only use one and a half times the amount of salt, depending on taste.

**Salt affects the crust**

Salt also affects the crust. Too much will make a tough crust. The right amount makes a crisp crust. It is hard to develop a crust at all without at least some salt.[3]

# LIQUIDS, SHORTENING, EGGS

**Liquids**

Since moisture is the catalyst for the development of both gluten and yeast, a liquid of some kind is essential for all risen breads.

**Water**

Water is the most common liquid. If the water is hard and has too many minerals, it will toughen the gluten and slow down the process of fermentation. Soft water, which is relatively free of minerals, softens the gluten and yields a sticky dough. Medium-hard water is the kind desirable for bread making, as it provides the minerals necessary to activate the yeast without either hardening or softening the gluten. If you must use hard water, boil it first to soften it. If you must use soft water, use a larger amount of salt to compensate for the mineral deficiency in the water. As with other fermented foods, the special qualities of various breads are often attributed to the local properties of the water, which might explain why certain breads are so difficult to imitate.

**Potato water**

Potato water (water in which potatoes have been boiled) has long had a reputation for making bread stay moist longer. As a matter of routine, pioneer women fixed potatoes for their families the day before baking bread. Do not neglect to use the cooking water of potatoes or of any other vegetables (or the blanching water from nuts or the soaking water from dried fruits) in your bread dough.

**Milk**

Milk prolongs the life of bread as well as making a smoother, softer, more cakelike crumb. You may use scalded and cooled whole milk or powdered dry milk. Whole milk *must* be scalded. This not only prevents the bacteria in it from interfering with the yeast, but is also a precaution against the overly soft dough that unscalded milk tends to produce. Though the troublesome ingredient in unheated milk has not been identified, it is related to the whey proteins and its effect is eliminated by heating.

Some bakers feel that powdered low-fat milk is preferable to fresh whole milk for reasons other than ease of preparation. Ada Lou Roberts, for example, claims that bread made with dried skim milk browns more evenly, develops a tenderer crust, and that "the crumb does not become hard and dry when cold as with fresh milk breads."[4] In addition, it is simple to double the amount of milk protein (by doubling the amount of milk powder) without increasing the amount of dough.

**Other liquids**

It is also possible and quite delightful to enhance the flavor of a particular bread by using, for all or part of the liquid, vegetable or fruit juices, purées, soup stock, soft cheeses, buttermilk, tofu, spiced tea, or beer.

*Note:* Whatever liquid you choose, be sure it is *lukewarm* (approximately 105°F) before you add the yeast to it.

**Shortening**

*Shortening* is the generic term for fat or oil added to dough. Fats, which are solid shortening, and oils, which are liquid, give bread "shortness," that is, the property of breaking and crushing easily. Either kind when added to dough makes a tender, flaky, richer tasting, and longer lasting bread. French bread, for example, which is hard to break and goes stale quickly, has little or no shortening. Although not at all *necessary* for bread, if your goal is a smooth crumb with good keeping qualities (the presence of shortening tends to lessen the amount of water lost through evaporation), the addition of some kind of shortening will help.

**When should shortening be added?**

When using a shortening, understand that its globules coat the grains of flour, forming a barrier that shuts out the liquid needed to form gluten. Simultaneously, shortening seals the yeast cells off from their source of nourishment. By making the outside of the cells slick, it makes their job of rising and supporting one another harder. Thus, fats or oils should be added to dough only after the interaction of flour, liquid, and yeast is well underway.

**Butter**

For baking use *fresh*, unsalted butter. Because it lacks salt (which acts as a preservative), "sweet" butter is slightly more perishable than salted butter. Buy it in small quantities or store it in your freezer. It is worth getting as salted butter not only contains salt, but also moisture absorbed by the salt and, quite possibly, food coloring, an additive rarely used in butter made simply from fresh, possibly raw, cream.

Butter and eggs are often used together as fats because egg whites, while acting as a leavener, coagulate during baking and tend to dry out a dough. Butter compensates for this drying and also softens the gluten. Since a softened gluten structure offers less resistance to gas given off by the growing yeast, a dough containing butter will rise high faster. The effect on the finished loaf can be quite dramatic depending on the quantity of butter and eggs used and also on *how* and *when* they are incorporated. Even a small amount, however, will give a bread a soft crust and moist, yellow interior.

**Incorporating butter into dough**

To make butter creamy enough to be incorporated easily, start with it at room temperature. Knead it on a cool surface until it is pliable but not sticky. Break it into small pieces and add it to the fully risen sponge just before incorporating the final amounts of flour.

**Other kinds of fat**

Lard, hydrogenated vegetable fats, and margarine are other forms of solid shortening and may be substituted for butter. I mention them for completeness, but do not recommend them for use in bread because of their inferior flavor.

**Oils**

Sesame, safflower, cotton seed, corn, peanut, hazelnut, walnut, and olive oil are all liquid sources of shortening. Here again the important thing to remember is freshness. This is essential when selecting an oil, particularly corn and walnut oils, that, when unrefined, can be very unstable. Three pieces of advice: try to use oils that you can buy fresh; refrigerate the oils you use for baking; know that of the unrefined oils, sesame and olive are the most stable and, despite their strong flavors (which go beautifully with some breads), may be preferable to blander tasting oils that are more likely to be rancid.

*Note:* Corn oil has a peculiarity: about five hours after being incorporated into a dough its flavor intensifies. If the dough is left to ripen overnight, however, the oil metabolizes and its flavor is absorbed. Thus for a more mellow taste, it is a good idea to allow for a long or overnight fermentation of dough containing corn oil.

**Eggs**

Eggs make a lighter, higher loaf with a more delicate crumb. They add a rich flavor to bread and supply a structure-building protein that helps it rise and keep well.

**How and when to add eggs**

You can separate the yolks and whites and beat air into them for extra rising effect, or add them together, beaten or unbeaten. For sweet-yeasted dough, just the yolks are preferable, though whole eggs can be substituted (one whole egg for every two yolks). Egg yolks will have a creamy consistency, will be pale yellow in color, and will fall in ribbons from the whisk when thoroughly beaten. Egg whites will yield a better volume at room temperature.

If you are adding eggs to a recipe that does not otherwise call for them, be sure to measure them first (five eggs = approximately one cup) and correspondingly decrease the total amount of liquid called for. When added to the other ingredients, eggs must always be at room temperature (so as not to cool the dough down) and for the same reasons as apply to other fats, they are best added in the second stage after the sponge has been set and allowed to rise.

**How many eggs?**

Eggs should be used sparingly as dough with a lot of eggs (particularly egg whites) tends to dry out more rapidly. When multiplying a recipe, you need not increase the number of eggs in the same proportion as you increase the flour. If you double a recipe calling for two eggs, for example, you might use three rather than four eggs.

**What kind of eggs?**

Consider the background of the egg and its freshness. An egg that floats in water is not fresh. Eggs that have recently hatched from organically fed, uninjected chickens are delicious and nourishing.

**Baking egg bread**

Because doughs with generous amounts of eggs (and butter) are more delicate, they are baked at a lower temperature for a longer time than doughs that have very little fat or none at all. The high moisture content of egg bread makes humidifying techniques unnecessary.

# EMBELLISHMENTS

Virtually any vegetable or fruit can be incorporated into bread dough for variety of color, taste, and texture without affecting the basic bread-making procedure.

**Raw vegetables**

A subtle, sometimes just perceptible effect is created by adding grated or finely chopped raw vegetables to bread. Because they are exceptionally moist, vegetables such as zucchini, eggplant, and cucumbers need to be shredded, salted, squeezed of excess liquid, and rinsed of the excess salt before being mixed in. Less watery vegetables can be used directly after grating. Add them at the sponge stage. The shreds will cook in the time it takes the loaf to bake.

**Fruit and vegetable purées**

Cooked vegetable or fruit purées will suffuse an entire loaf with flavor and color. Winter squash, root vegetables such as beets, parsnips, rutabagas, Jerusalem artichokes, and sweet potatoes, apple or tomato sauce, and purées made from cranberries, papaya, avocado, pears, quince, etc., are delicious. Being incorporated at the sponge stage, a purée may possibly replace all the liquid in the recipe. Be sure to cool purées to lukewarm before adding them.

**Cooked whole grains**

Cooked and cooled whole grains, such as rice, oats, millet, and barley, beans or legumes of all kinds, and spreads such as tahini and peanut butter add moisture, texture, and wonderful flavor to bread. Because of their weight they are best added either as you knead the dough after the sponge has risen, or when you are shaping the loaf.

**Dry cereals**

Granola, shredded wheat and other whole grain dry cereals (even graham cracker crumbs) will lend nutritional and textural variations to your bread. For maximum crunchiness, add them when you are shaping the loaf.

**Nutritional supplements**

If you so desire, bread can be an easy way of incorporating supplements such as bone meal powder, brewers' yeast, dolomite, etc., into your family's diet.

| | |
|---|---|
| **Soft cheese** | Soft cheeses, such as ricotta, pot cheese, cottage cheese, or very young goat cheeses (fromage blanc or chabis) are moist enough to be treated as all or part of the liquid. |
| **Hard cheese** | Hard cheeses must be grated to disperse well. If added to the dough when it is first mixed, they will lose their textural identity in the kneading process and eventually suffuse the bread. Since hard cheeses tend to have a high fat content (which acts on the dough much like butter), it is preferable to add them after the dough has risen. Do this in two stages (adding and mixing, adding and mixing), to ensure an even distribution. The shreds of cheese will remain intact, appearing as melted nuggets in the finished loaf. |
| **Dried fruit, nuts, and seeds**  | Dried fruit and fresh nuts or seeds can be added to dough in quantities up to twice the weight of the dough itself. The fruit may be soaked in rum, brandy, or a fruit liqueur to enhance the flavor. Roasting nuts first in a slow oven till they are lightly browned develops their flavor and makes them crunchier. Blanching (steeping in boiling water for ten minutes) will remove skins and salt, giving the nuts a more delicate taste and finer texture. (Strain, cool, and return the steeping water to the bread. You may decrease the initial amount of salt if you think the dissolved salt from the nuts will make the bread too salty.) |
| | Because their extra bulk will hamper the dough's ability to rise, fruit and nuts are best added after the dough has risen, ideally when the loaf is shaped. Alternately, the dough can be treated like a platform, with these or other embellishments displayed on top. |
| **Sweeteners** | Sweeteners, perhaps the most controversial embellishment, are often added to doughs ostensibly to enhance their flavor. Always remember that when allowed to ripen fully, fresh flour, water, and salt by themselves produce a bread with a subtle natural sweetness, and that flour already, by itself, contains enough food for yeast to grow. It is a myth that yeast needs an additional sweetener to become active. The addition of the usual teaspoon of sugar when proofing yeast is primarily intended to speed up the action of the yeast so that you will know right away if it is alive. This is for *your* benefit. |
| | Sweeteners do act as a natural preservative and add interest and delicacy to bread when used with discretion. |

Certain grains seem to love certain sweeteners and the flavor and effect of other embellishments can be balanced by the correct sweetener. Some sweeteners have a lot of food value.

Sugar has none, but it is light and sometimes worth using for a lack of an alternative. Honey is delicious in bread and has valuable enzymes and minerals though, when heated to the degree necessary for baking, it loses some of its nutritional value. Since it helps the bread hold moisture, breads made with honey tend to stay fresh longer. Because honey does not ferment as quickly as molasses, malt syrup, or sugar, doughs made with honey can be left to rise longer and will develop a fuller flavor. Some honeys are too powerful for bread. Be careful to select a honey (clover or alfalfa are mild; sunflower, buckwheat, and avocado are pungent) that will harmonize with the rest of your ingredients.

Heat does not destroy the nutrients in maple syrup, which is a good substitute for honey if the flavor is suitable. Molasses, particularly blackstrap molasses (though it has a strong taste), contains B vitamins and minerals, including iron. Other possible sweeteners are barley and wheat malt (which is the sprouted grain left overnight in a 200°F oven and then pulverized), malt extract syrup (to be found in natural food markets) and, as we have seen, fruit and dried fruit of all kinds.

Feel free to omit a sweetener altogether from any yeasted bread recipe. Just bear in mind that the less sweetener you use, the more rising time you should allow. This is to give the yeast more time to feed from the natural sweeteners in the grain.

**Herbs**

Herbs may be added early or late but, if you are concerned that their pungency might become overwhelming (herbs gain pungency with time), add them late to the risen dough. Fresh herbs should be stripped of their stems and chopped fine. Dried herbs should be crushed to release all of their oils.

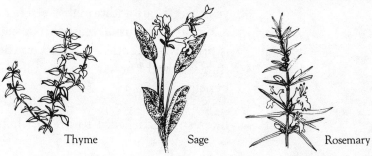

Thyme          Sage          Rosemary

**Spices**

As much as possible, use freshly ground whole spices. Because the flavor oils in ground spices dissipate rapidly, a more pungent taste will result if you grind whole spices yourself. Specialty or gourmet markets, specialty cookware stores, and coffee, tea, and spice shops will sell spices in bulk, either whole or ground. Buying in bulk is preferable to buying prepackaged varieties: you get better and fresher spices without paying for the jar. Store spices for no more than three months in jars with tight lids or tight-fitting stoppers away from direct sun. Light tends to evaporate the aromatic oils that give spices their liveliness. Heat robs them of flavor and dampness may cake them. Because spices are highly perishable, they are best purchased in small quantities.

*Note:* Displaying spices on a spice rack in a sunny, cheerful kitchen is a pretty, but impractical way of preserving them. A cupboard or drawer near your work space is preferable.

**Leftovers**

Leftovers may be used in your bread in imaginative combinations. Add between half and one and a quarter cups per loaf after the dough has risen. Chances are if you liked the meal that was leftover (spaghetti), you will love the bread made from it (spaghetti bread). Besides, this is a very economical way to order your kitchen.

# Part II

# METHODS AND PRINCIPLES OF BREAD MAKING

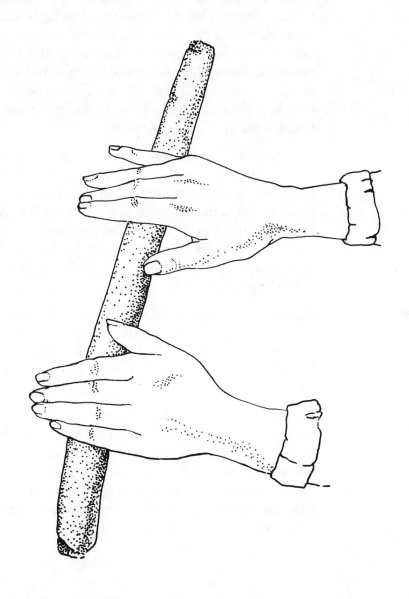

# DOUGH

**You are in control**

The point cannot be stressed enough that bread making is an art replete with choices. You can slow it down or hurry it up, overbake for a crunchy crust or over-rise for a chewy loaf with big holes. The correct thing is what you want. You are in control and, if you understand what bread is about, you can tailor any dough to suit your exact specifications.

**The ideal dough**

Primarily you are after a mature, ripe, well-developed, piquant flavor. This is why you are baking bread at home. Such flavor, along with a fine even texture (crumb), is achieved through long slow risings. No short-rising technique, or chemical, or fancy machinery can duplicate what dough can do on its own, if just allowed to. Bread takes time to make but it is the *bread's* time, not yours. Actually bread takes very little of your time.

**Rising**

The question of time, upon which the growth and maturity of the dough depend, is a crucial one. As Walter Banfield says, "Trying to beat the time factor to get premature maturity is a most common cause of poor bread."[5] Unavoidably, certain changes must be effected in dough before any attempt is made to stop its growth by baking. When all of these changes have been undergone, the dough is considered ripe.

**Ripeness**

Ripeness, however, is variable. Different flours require different amounts of ripening time. Whatever the amount, it cannot be meddled with. If a certain flour requires four hours to ripen, for example, it must be given four hours. It will not be ripe in two.

For a dough to achieve ripeness, the following changes must take place: The protein fabric of the flour must be "conditioned;" flavor-producing substances must be developed; the acidity of the dough, which influences volume and flavor, must be developed within fine limits; and conditions must be right to ensure the correct gas production in the final stage.

**Ripening**

Though rising is an *indication* that ripening is taking place, it is not a *measure* of the degree of ripeness. A dough, for example, may come up to a given level in its first rise, but even though this level may be high, the dough would not be ripe at this point.

**Under-ripeness**

Dough as it ferments becomes lighter and brighter. If, once it is baked, a bread shows a poor color, a crumb with an open grain, or large holes, the dough was probably under-ripe.

**Gluten: Bread muscles**

Fortunately, there are innumerable short cuts to save yourself time without compromising the maturity of the dough. In employing any of them, realize that the texture of the bread will get finer and finer each time the dough rises. (Thus, for coarse-grained bread, you actually want a short-rise method.) If you think of the gluten fibers as a muscular network, you will understand that the more they stretch and flex in growing, the more finely tuned will be their springiness. Thus, at any time you wish, you can stop what you are doing, punch the dough down (relieving it of the yeast's gaseous by-products) and, depending on the temperature of the place you put it, it will rise again, either slowly or quickly, receiving great benefit in the process. If you suddenly have to leave your dough, punch it down (see page 49) and place it in the refrigerator. The quality and flavor of your loaf will only be enhanced by the extra chance this gives the gluten to stretch and develop.

**Temperature**

Because yeast is a living plant, it is necessary to consider the ecology of the environment in which you intend to grow it. Like sprouts, yeast wants a warm, dark, moist environment. This means that rinsing your bowl with hot water and drying it with a towel and warming your flour briefly in a low oven will be beneficial. You must use warm water (between 100° and 105°F) and the dough itself will generate its own heat as the yeast grows. Consequently (except for doughs with a lot of butter, eggs, and sugar, which do require special warmth), you do not have to be too fussy about finding a cove for your dough. Ordinary room temperatures are fine. Remember, it is *desirable* that risings be lengthy.

**Higher temperatures**

Should you choose to use a temperature higher than that of an ordinary room (which is between 60° and 75°F), as a means of quickening the rising process, bear in mind that the warmth should *surround* the bowl of dough. If it comes from one direction only, for instance, from underneath, as from a radiator or from one side, as from an open fire, the dough will start to cook and form a crust on the hot side. Provided the yeast is still alive, you can save dough to which this has happened by punching it down, cutting away the crust, kneading it again, and setting it to rise again in a cooler spot or one where the heat is more evenly distributed. Here are some suggested specially warm places: a warm steamy bathroom, a prewarmed electric oven (turn it on to "warm" for a few minutes and then turn it off) with either the light left on or a pan of just-boiled water on the lowest shelf, the top of a gas stove near but not touching the pilot light, a rack over another bowl or over a sink containing warm water, or the top of a warm radio or a hot water tank.

**Lower temperatures**

Another, far preferable, paractice is to *lower* the temperature of the area in which your bread will rise. This is wonderful for dough, giving it plenty of time, and allows you to make your bread at intervals as widely spaced as several days.

**Refrigeration**

Cool temperatures retard both yeast growth and gluten formation (which is why ice water and long rests in the refrigerator are prescribed for flaky, but not for glutenous dough). They do not stop growth, but relax and slow it in such a way that the yeast's activity will continue for as long as twenty-four hours. If the dough is periodically punched down and re-oiled (to renew its air and prevent a crust from encasing it), it can be kept in the refrigerator for up to four days with excellent results. One can set a sponge and refrigerate it until one is ready to continue. A fully prepared dough can be kneaded and then refrigerated to slow the fermentation. Unbaked loaves can be refrigerated and go directly into the oven. Dough refrigerated before shaping must first come to room temperature (a process that can take three or four hours) before being kneaded, rested, and shaped.

Seal the bowl or pans in which you have sponge or dough with plastic. The bowl should be large enough to allow room for triple expansion. The plastic around the loaf pans also should not be so tight as to inhibit the loaf's growth. A lightly floured, tied plastic bag is quite suitable.

**Freezing**

Freezing will stop the yeast's action completely. If you are planning to freeze an unbaked loaf, prepare the dough with double the amount of yeast, proof the yeast (see page 27) and then use a cold liquid for your main moisture. Knead well, allow the dough to rest, and shape it into loaves. Finally, see that it is well wrapped before freezing for up to eight or nine months.

Freezing does not have to be planned, however, and dough may be frozen at any time after it has risen once. Seal the dough or preshaped loaves carefully before freezing and allow them to thaw *thoroughly* afterwards.

**Water rising**

Bread dough can be mixed, wrapped loosely in a cloth and immersed in a bowl of cold water for anywhere from two hours to all day or night. Soon it will rise to the top of the bowl and look, as Elizabeth David puts it, like a "lovely fat soft pillow." Unwrap it, punch it down, and knead in the ordinary way. The dough does not stick to the cloth and is not more difficult to knead, though it will be somewhat moister than dough raised in the usual way.

This system is very useful in warm weather when dough might become overfermented. It has the advantage over refrigeration of saving you from having to return the dough to room temperature before kneading and shaping it into loaves. Advocates feel that water rising produces a moist, well-expanded, very tender bread.

**Has it risen enough?**

Properly risen dough approximately doubles (occasionally triples) its original size. To know for sure if your dough has risen enough, make an indentation in it with two fingers. If the rising process has fully stretched it, the dough should not spring back.

**Altitude**

Rising goes more quickly in higher altitudes. If you are at a high altitude and want to give your dough its full maturation time, use less yeast, refrigerate it for some of the time, and emphasize more rising periods of shorter duration rather than fewer ones of longer duration.

## Kneading

Once the oil, salt, and some additional flour have been added to the sponge and the mass is becoming a dough, turn it out of its bowl onto a lightly floured surface and let it rest for a few minutes while you butter or oil the bowl. You do not have to wash it. Allow the stray, as yet uncongealed flour in the dough bowl to be the first flour that you knead in. Thus you will avoid inadvertently adding too much flour before you know exactly how much you will need.

Marble or wood provide ideal surfaces for kneading. The height of the surface in relation to your own height is particularly important. You want to be able to push the dough comfortably, but with force. Be sure you are not hampered in your movements. Some people find it easier to put a bread board on the floor and kneel down, in the Indian fashion.

Kneading homogenizes the ingredients in dough and stretches and strengthens its gluten mesh. Doughs with flours low in gluten will be stickier and absorb more flour in the kneading process. All doughs absorb some flour, however, so hold out some of the flour called for in the recipe and add it, if necessary, when you are kneading.

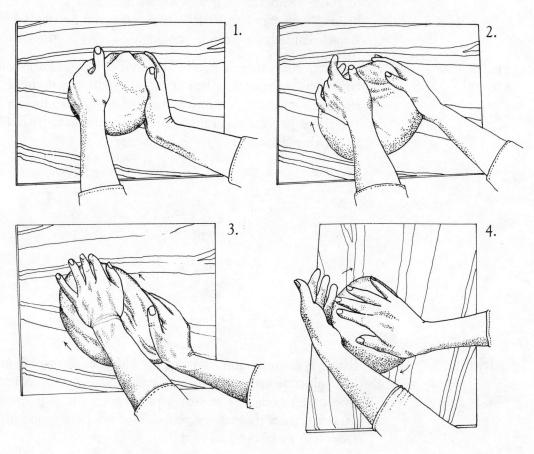

To knead, pick up the far edge of the dough and fold it toward you. Push down and forward with the heels of your hands as you rock forward with your whole body. Turn the dough one quarter turn while rocking back and fold and push again with another forward motion. Gradually the folding and pushing will become one movement and the dough will congeal as flour is added to the board and to the top surface as needed to keep it from sticking. To prevent *excessive* stickiness and to avoid adding too much flour, work with sharp, quick, on-and-off movements. Never let the dough lounge in your hands. This process will take between ten and twenty minutes, depending on the consistency and quantity of your dough.

**Overkneading**

It is not possible to overknead unless you are using a mixer with a dough hook, in which case choose a low speed and watch carefully. When it reaches the consistency of your ear-lobe, it is done. Overkneading will result in overdeveloping and possibly destroying the gluten and, finally, in a tough loaf of bread.

*Note:* There is no difference in the protein value of more or less developed gluten.

**Test for well-kneaded dough**

Underkneading is the more common problem. To be sure your dough is kneaded enough, make an indentation in it with your finger. Since by now, one hopes, you will have fully exercised your dough, charging the gluten (muscle) fibers with energy, the resulting hole should vanish (pop right back). Eventually you will be able to feel and respond to the satisfied springiness in a dough that has received sufficient kneading.

**Punching down**

Dough *can* over-rise. Too much rising pushes the elasticity in the gluten to its limit, sometimes causing it to break. Once the glutenous fibers are broken, they cannot be reunited. The resulting loaf will be coarse and heavy.

Punching down is a way to stop this instantly. Punching down is just what it says. Use your fists. Punch *hard* down into the center of the dough and keep punching with both fists consecutively until all the air is released.

**Autointoxication**

Consequent to over-rising is a state called *autointoxication*. This happens when the carbon dioxide and alcohol build up so extensively that the yeast suffocates and expires in its own waste. Punching down and kneading dough disseminates its gaseous by-products, freshening its air and reinvigorating it so that it will stretch and grow again without toxicity.

# MOLDING

**Bread dough before shaping**

A magnified cross section of bread dough just before it is shaped into loaves should reveal a delicate foam of gas-filled gluten pockets. To protect this fragile internal structure and so as not to break its *invisible* elastic skin, it is important to be very gentle now as you stretch the dough. Even with careful handling, some of the pockets will inevitably collapse. This is why the shaped loaves are allowed to rise once more before being baked. Before shaping the loaves, cut the dough into pieces of the size that you want. For free-formed loaves, there is considerable leeway in estimating the volume of dough per loaf, but, for loaf pans, the measurement must be more exact if the loaf is to have a good appearance. Too little dough will produce a stunted loaf; too much will become top-heavy. The right amount will fill about two-thirds of the pan. If you have a kitchen scale, you will find that between one and three-quarters and two pounds of dough will usually be adequate for the standard 4½-by-8½-inch loaf pan. As some doughs are heavier than others, these quantities may vary.

Allow the pieces of dough to rest for about five minutes, using the time, if you wish, to oil the pans. If you are making a lot of loaves, you may wish to dust the surface on which the mounds of dough rest with white rice flour. This is rich in starch, but slow to absorb liquids and will prevent the dough from sticking.

Knead each piece of dough before shaping it.

**Oiling and buttering pans**

It is a good idea to have one brush that you use just for buttering or oiling breadpans and another, separate one, for glazing. Choose your pan and, unless it is teflon, butter or oil it lightly. Many bakers prefer butter. The crust will imbibe its flavor and butter does not burn easily during the baking process. If you are using oil and oiling more than one pan, pour a little into the first pan, brush it around, and then brush the excess into the second pan, and so forth, brushing the oil remaining in the final pan back into the jar.

**Bread dough after shaping**

After shaping, cover the dough with a damp cloth and let it rise until the center of the loaf is level with or just *barely* rises above the top edge of the pan. This will happen in a shorter period of time than any of the previous risings. *Never* let the dough over-rise at this stage. If you do, when it bakes, either its center will sink or its top will be billowy and full of holes, with a tendency to break off entirely from its too-densely textured bottom. When you see that a loaf has risen more than slightly over the top ridge, it is better to remove it, punch it down, reshape it, and let it rise properly. For free-formed loaves, do not let them rise by more than about a third again.

**Handmade irregularities**

Homemade bread *should* look homemade. Small irregularities add charm and character. So long as the form serves your purpose and does not reflect some serious defect in the bread-making process, your bread should look as if it has been made by *you*.

## Shaping Techniques—Pan Bread

Here are a few shaping techniques that you might like to try.

**Let the pan do the shaping**

The method I have always used and invariably return to is that of allowing the pan to do most of the work. First, knead your portion of dough briefly. It will firm up quickly.

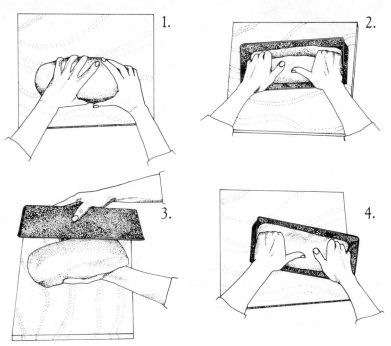

As it does, gently ease it into a log shape. This is more or less an extension of the kneading motion. You do not need to roll it out with a pin, like pie dough, and then roll it up again. Place this log seam-side *up* into a greased loaf pan, press firmly into the corners and floor, turn it upside-down so that the dough falls into your hand, and return it this time with what was the bottom side facing up. The pan thus gives the surface a symmetrically shaped, smooth, professional look.

**Double loaf** If you cut the dough for one loaf in half, you can form two mounds and place them upright in a standard greased loaf pan side by side. When they bake, the mounds grow together and brace each other, tending to rise higher than they would otherwise. This also increases the surface crust, which many feel is the best part of bread.

**Bun bread** Divide the dough for one loaf into approximately two-ounce portions. Shape each portion into a ball and place the balls in a zigzag pattern along the bottom of a prepared loaf pan. Do not be afraid to squeeze them together. The finished bread will resemble a loaf of buns. If you use a wreath-shaped pan, you will have a wreath of buns.

**Roly-poly** Cut the dough for one loaf into nine or ten equal-sized pieces. Roll each piece into a cylinder one inch in diameter and the length of the width of your loaf pan. Arrange the cylinders adjacently across the bottom of the pan, pressing them closely together. They will rise and make a wavy crust.

**Pan braid** Dividing dough for one loaf into three strands and braiding them is a common shaping technique. Usually the resulting braid is placed on a baking sheet to become a somewhat low, wide bread. (For a free-form variation, see instructions for a layered braid, page 55.) The braid, however, can as easily be put into a greased loaf pan. It will rise as a normal loaf and the seed and nuts traditionally used as toppings on such twists will stick better on the uneven surface. Braid from the center out. Then pinch each end and tuck it under.

**Ring shapes** Once you braid or twist your strands, you can also press the two ends together, making a circle. Bake this circle on a baking sheet or place it inside a tube pan to prevent it from spreading. If using the former, place a small ring in the center hole or be sure to widen it with your fingers before putting it in the oven. This is a particularly pleasing shape for doughs containing vegetable or fruit purées.

**One-pound loaf pans** For individual servings or for small amounts of dough left over after shaping larger loaves, do not neglect these charming tiny pans.

**Monkey bread** Finally, there are the bubble breads that do very well in flower pots (see page 75 for the correct way to bake with flower pots), charlotte molds, or bundt pans—anything round and deep. There is a special recipe for Monkey Bread (page 122) but if your intention is really to serve a warm bread more or less as you would rolls or buns, rather than in slices, any dough can be broken off into small pieces, rolled between your palms into balls, rolled, or not, in melted butter or a mixture of melted butter, brown cinnamon-sugar, and currants, and placed randomly in your greased pan. Do not fill it too full. Another method is to place the balls in the pan in layers and pour the butter, etc., over each layer. Either way, the resulting mound of "bubbles" can be placed hot in the center of a table, and everyone simply pulls off the little portions.

# Hearth Loaves

**Round loaves** Round loaves can also be achieved with your cupped hands. Form a portion of dough into a mound as high or low as you like. Some breads look well when shaped

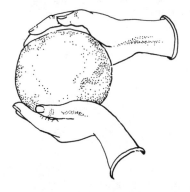

like little mountains; others look better in a flat shape. The same technique may be used to make a slightly elongated loaf.

**Little wooden bowls**

If you have a basket of the right shape, you can line it with cloth and set your mound in it upside down, using the cloth to cover the top of the dough. When it has risen sufficiently, simply turn the loaf right side up onto your baking sheet or tiles.

French bakers flour little wooden bowls like salad bowls and press portions of dough into them. The warmth of wood is conducive to the growth of yeast. As it rises, the loaves are simply turned from the bowls onto a baking sheet that has been greased or sprinkled with meal or flour. Even better is to bake your rounded loaves on preheated clay tiles. The hot surface makes them plump immediately, setting the crust so that they will hold their full height instead of spreading as uncontained free-formed loaves tend to do.

**Wreaths** There are two techniques for making wreaths. Either, take the dough for one wreath, flatten it, and press a hole through the center with your thumb. Rotate the wreath slowly so that your hands can smooth the outer edges and enlarge the center hole to a diameter of approximately three inches. Or, roll the dough for one wreath into a strand between eighteen and twenty-four inches long. Curve it into a circle, overlapping and pinching the ends together.

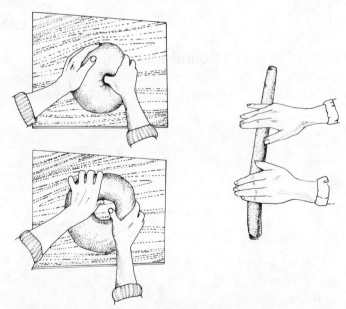

**Snail shell** Roll the dough for one loaf into a cylinder approximately twelve inches long. Coil it tightly from the center out, pinching and tucking the end under.

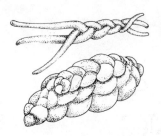

**Layered braid** Divide the dough for one large loaf into three groups of three strands, each group being progressively larger. Braid each group from the center out and then layer them so that the smallest braid is on top. This layering of varying sized braids makes a sumptuous presentation.

**False braid** Roll the dough for one loaf out to the length you would like your braid and to three times the width. Cut equidistant diagonal fingers a third of the way in on both sides. Butter each finger and fold it across the center, lapping the fingers alternately so as to mock a woven pattern.

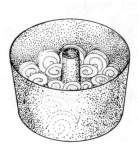

**Breakfast clusters** Divide the dough for one loaf into two parts and roll each into a ten-by-ten-inch square. Brush the squares with butter and sprinkle them with filling. Roll each square tightly like a jelly roll and pinch it to secure the edges. Then slice it into one-inch rounds. Begin to arrange the slices around the bottom of a buttered ten-inch tube pan. Each slice should be touching the next. Place another group of slices vertically around the pan, and then a third group straddling the first. Continue straddling slices until all are used. What results is a loaf built of individual swirls.

# SLITTING AND GLAZING

**Slitting loaves**

Most loaves before they are put in the oven should be decoratively slit in two or three places with a sharp knife or razor blade. Because the outside of the loaf cooks first, thereby creating more or less of a shell, the growth of the expanding yeast cells, which are still alive in the center, is hampered. Slits allow the release of this outward pressure, giving the dough room to form a paler and more delicate secondary crust. They also vent internal moisture.

*Note:* Because the gluten structure in rye flour is more delicate, make fewer and shallower slits when working with rye flour breads.

**Watch the angle**

The angle at which the cut is made influences the development of the loaf. Be sure your cutting edge is not drawn vertically but at an angle toward the horizontal. You do not have to cut deep.

**Patterns for slits**

The way a loaf of bread is slit affects both its appearance and the nature of its crust. Indeed, many bakers become famous for a certain loaf of bread that differs from other similar loaves primarily in the way in which it is slit. Patterns are endless and each will leave its distinctive mark. Here are some ideas.

## Slits for pan breads

One slit down the center with four or five diagonal cuts radiating on either side. A series of diagonal cuts.

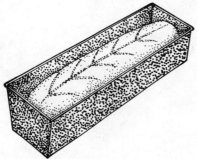
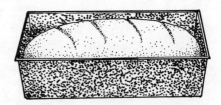

# Slits for round loaves

Four slightly diagonal lines across the top of loaf in one direction and four more in the opposite direction, forming a grid.

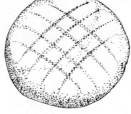

Three to five lines cut in one direction only.

Two slightly diagonal lines across the top of the loaf in one direction and two more in the opposite direction, forming a tic-tac-toe design.

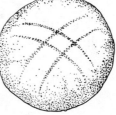

Cut a circle around the circumference of the top of the round for a bubble effect.

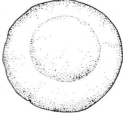

Slash a single line across the center top of the loaf. This gives the effect of dividing the loaf into two.

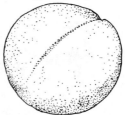

A similar effect is created by tying a string all the way around the center of a loaf when it is put on the baking sheet to rise. As the bread expands, the string holds the crease. In the oven the crust breaks along this line.

Slash a triangle of three curved lines that cross over one another at the ends.

The same can be done with a square. There will be four lines and four corner crosses.

On top of the loaf slash an X extending the ends to a point halfway down the sides.

A star may be made of eight lines radiating from the top of the loaf down the sides to within one inch of the baking sheet.

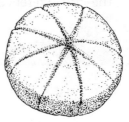

A modified star may be made with four radiating lines that quarter the bread from the top of the loaf to within one inch of the bottom edge. Within each quarter, midway between cuts is a short, two-inch diagonal slit.

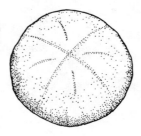

## Slits for elongated loaves

Beginning near one end, cut lines at one-inch intervals widthwise across the top of the loaf for a banded effect.

Run six slits the length of the loaf beginning and ending at a point several inches in from the ends.

## Slits for wreaths

Cut a circle around the top of the wreath midway between the circumference and the center hole.

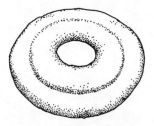

Cut three connecting lines to form a triangle around the center hole. Curve each line to allow the ends to overlap and form an X.

## Glazing and glazes

Slitting and glazing are usually done at the same time, just before the loaves go in the oven. Most yeasted breads benefit from a glaze that gives them a finished look and prevents the crust from becoming dried out or tough. Many breads can simply be brushed with an egg wash (one egg beaten with one teaspoon of water) or any one of the following glazes just before baking. Or, you can brush the loaves with water as you remove them from the oven. There are many different glazes for bread, each one slightly different. If you are afraid the glaze will over-brown, apply it about fifteen minutes before the end of baking.

If you have a brush for oiling your loaf pans, use a separate one for glazing the loaves. Reserve these two brushes solely for their respective purposes.

# Glazing Chart

| | |
|---|---|
| Plain water | Crusty surface |
| 1 egg + pinch salt | Shiny surface |
| 1 egg + 1 teaspoon milk | Shiny medium glaze |
| 1 egg + 2 tablespoons water | Less intense shiny golden surface |
| 1 egg yolk + 1 teaspoon water | Shiny golden crust |
| 1 egg yolk + 1-1/2 teaspoons cream | Shiny brown crust |
| Egg white | Crisp, light-colored crust |
| 1 egg white + 1 teaspoon water | Sticky surface for holding seeds |
| 1 egg white + 1 teaspoon milk | Shiny transparent glaze |
| Melted butter | Velvety finish |
| Molasses | Mahogany crust |
| Dusting flour | Powdery finish (flour causes the surface to dry quickly, producing a firm, chewy crust) |
| 1 tablespoon cornstarch + 2 tablespoons water | Hard crust. Apply several times during baking |
| 1/4 cup water + 1/4 cup sugar | Clear glaze for sweet rolls and breakfast breads |

*Any of these glazes can be topped with a sprinkling of nuts or seeds. Poppy and sesame seeds are frequently used. Try black caraway or irigoma, a Japanese roasted sesame seed.*

# BAKING

## Know Your Oven

Ovens tend to have definite personalities. Some bake high; some bake low. Thermostats are frequently inaccurate. It is important for a baker to be cognizant of each idiosyncrasy. Keep two thermometers in your oven. If they agree, you will *know* its temperature.

To insure uniformity, air must be allowed to circulate freely around your bread. Examine your finished loaves carefully. Poorly distributed heat can cause an uneven shape or crumb or *shelling*, which occurs when the bread underneath the top crust separates and forms a tunnel down the length of the loaf. This is usually caused when either the top surface of the dough partially dries out during rising and the heat of the oven is not able to penetrate this thick surface or "shell" uniformly, or when the oven temperature is too low and the dough expands unevenly. If one part of your oven is hotter than another, don't leave one loaf there for the whole time. If necessary during baking, switch your loaves around, possibly twice, though once is usually enough.

**Baking temperatures**

Just about any bread can be baked successfully in a regular oven at 350°F for between thirty-five and fifty minutes, depending on its size and density.

Elizabeth David suggests a method of simulating an old-fashioned slackening oven in which a loaf might have been surrounded by hot coals and allowed to remain in the oven as the coals cooled off. One would place the loaf in the center of a 425°F oven for the first ten minutes, reduce the heat to 400°F for the next ten to fifteen minutes, and finally lower it to 350°F until the loaf is baked.

## Developing Hard Crusts

Elizabeth David's method is particularly effective if you want a hard crust, as an initially hot oven will develop a crust quickly by setting the gluten before the loaf is fully baked. Humidity will delay the drying and setting of a crust, thereby giving the dough a chance to expand more fully before this happens. That is one of the reasons professional bakers use steam jets.

**The purpose of steam**

Other reasons for using steam are that steam encourages the dough to bulge where it was slit with a knife or razor; that a moist oven favors the caramelization of sugar in dough to give a golden color and glossy appearance to the crust; and that successive steaming glosses over the dusty, pale look that the dry air of a typical home oven sets.

**How to create steam**

Steam is created naturally when the oven's heat penetrates the dough. Therefore, the important time for manufacturing steam is at the beginning of the baking period. Place a pan of hot water on the floor of a gas oven or the bottom shelf of an electric oven while it is being preheated, and pour more boiling water into the pan as you put the loaves in. This will create an initial tremendous burst of steam. Alternately, you can spray the loaves with an atomizer once every five minutes during the first twenty minutes of baking or until the crust begins to brown, if this is sooner. Once the crust has formed, turn the oven down and stop spraying. The bread should finish baking in a dry oven.

**Another method for hard crusts**

Another method for developing a firm crust is to remove a loaf from its pan during the final stages of baking and place it on its side either directly on the oven shelf, or, if you have them, on clay tiles spread on a lower shelf. The porous tiles help to distribute heat more evenly and will also absorb moisture from beneath a loaf placed directly on them to insure a crunchy bottom crust. A dark colored carbon-steel baking sheet will also absorb heat to crisp the bottom of the loaves.

If your crust turns out *too* hard, you can soften it by leaving the loaf in a plastic bag overnight.

# Developing Soft Crusts

For a soft crust you want a slower, steadier oven and, as you remove the loaves, brush them with milk, cream, or melted butter. An even softer crust will result if you wrap a tea towel around the loaves as they cool. Milk in dough makes for a soft crust. Doughs containing sugar or milk brown more rapidly and need to be baked at lower temperatures anyway. Hardly any crust at all will form on pullman loaves, those baked in the rectangular pans with lids. See Glazes and Glazing, page 60, for other ways in which to vary your crusts.

**Is it done yet?**

Loaves achieve their final size in the oven. Often, in fact, they will increase in size by a third during the first few minutes of baking. This initial spurt of growth is known as "oven spring" and it will last until the interior temperature of the loaf reaches 140°F. At this point the yeast cells die. The crust will be completely formed.

The best way to know when a loaf is done is to become familiar with the particular characteristics of a particular dough, and to have *seen* what it looks like when it is thoroughly baked.

**The "hollow" sound**

Tapping the loaf for its characteristic "hollow" sound is another, but much less reliable, test. There are several reasons for this. Different doughs have different sounds. As a bread progresses from stage to stage in the oven, its own characteristic sound will vary. The sound that is most striking (the one ubiquitously referred to as the "hollow" sound), develops during the last quarter of the baking period. If you know your bread, you will soon come to know its version of this special sound. Then you can use it as a double check.

To check for the hollow sound, remove the loaf from its pan and tap the bottom crust lightly. You should hear a sound like an echo from the inside. Because the top of the loaf has been more fully exposed to the oven's heat, a tap on the top does not provide as accurate a picture of the loaf's center as a tap on the bottom.

At the same time the sides of the loaf should hold up on their own and not be too soft. The color of the bread should be rich and complete.

Always test for doneness about five or ten minutes before the earliest time suggested in the recipe to allow for variables.

# Cooling

When a loaf is taken from the oven, it still contains a lot of moisture in the form of steam, that it needs to lose as it cools. Therefore, it is essential that the loaf be removed from the pan immediately before this steam, which cann͑ escape, condenses and makes the bread soggy.

As soon as you remove your loaves from the oven and from their pans, place them either on a rack, so that air can circulate entirely around them, or across the still hot, empty loaf pans. The latter method allows for a more gradual temperature change.

Be sure to allow the loaves to cool completely, which will take about three hours, before storing them. Despite the wonderful smell, bread is not easily digested immediately after it is removed from the oven.

# STORAGE

## Keeping Bread Fresh

Points to remember:

The larger the loaf, the longer it will stay fresh.

Darker breads and denser breads, as well as breads with moist or rich embellishments, stay fresh longer than light, airy ones.

Never wrap a loaf until it is *completely* cool (about three hours after it emerges from the oven).

Bread keeps best if it is allowed to breathe. Therefore, a plastic bag is not ideal in that moisture naturally released from the loaf condenses in the stifled atmosphere. The crust softens and eventually a mold will form. A clean dry place at room temperature or a little cooler—some houses still have old-fashioned coolers—is what you are looking for. A paper bag or the traditional bread box or bread drawer in which the bread is placed, *unwrapped*, is perfect.

Although studies by flour companies have shown that bread stored in the refrigerator actually goes stale faster than bread at room temperature, refrigeration will delay mold, if a loaf is to be kept for more than a few days and you decide against freezing it.

When a loaf starts to go stale, slice it, freeze the slices, and then toast each slice as you need it.

Bread will freshen if you heat it in a 350°F oven for about fifteen minutes.

## Freezing Bread

Points to remember:

If bread must be stored, the deep freeze is probably the best place. If left to cool thoroughly and then carefully sealed, a loaf will retain all its moisture and, when thawed, be *almost* indistinguishable from freshly made bread. The crust tends to suffer a little, however, so this method is more suitable to breads that have a larger diameter than baguettes, for example.

Properly wrapped loaves can be frozen for three or four months without losing flavor.

Breads embellished with nuts, fruits, and spices *improve* from storage periods, including freezing.

To freeze bread, allow it to cool thoroughly. Then, either wrap it in aluminum foil or place it in a medium to heavy plastic bag and tie it securely. Label and date it.

*Never* put a loaf directly from the oven into the freezer.

The sooner that the loaf is put into the freezer after it has cooled, the fresher it will remain. The idea is to lose as little moisture as possible.

To thaw: Keep the loaf inside the *unopened* foil or plastic bag. Frost particles inside the bag represent moisture that you want the bread to reabsorb. Normally a loaf will take two or three hours to thaw out at room temperature. When the moisture disappears, remove the bread and heat it in a 350°F oven for about ten or fifteen minutes. This will freshen the bread and firm the crust.

One can speed up the thawing process by putting the loaf still in its wrappings in a low oven (250°F) for half an hour when it is just about, but not quite, thawed, or by unwrapping it and transferring it straight from the freezer to a 300°F oven for between twenty-five and forty minutes, depending on its size. For immediate use, rebaking will, if anything, improve the bread.

For slicing, especially thin slices, a slightly under-thawed loaf is an advantage.

Slicing a loaf before it is frozen has several advantages: it greatly saves thawing time; you can pry apart the required number of slices and reheat them quickly, allowing the rest of the loaf to remain undisturbed; and, if you keep several kinds of sliced bread in your freezer, you may enjoy slices from a different kind at each meal.

# Part III

# GUIDELINES FOR EQUIPMENT

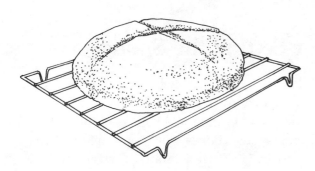

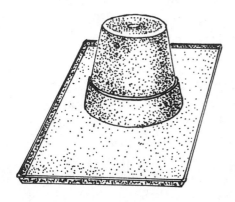

# GUIDELINES FOR EQUIPMENT

Bread baking does not require a lot of equipment. As a matter of fact, it is fun to go into an unsuspecting kitchen and improvise breads with whatever is at hand. Use what you have. But check first to make sure that all your utensils, including your oven, are impeccably clean. Then choose a working area that is spacious so that you can assemble your supplies first. To help determine your needs, what follows is a list of baking items and some guidelines to consider in shopping and caring for them.

## For Setting the Sponge

**Large bowl**

The traditional brown ceramic bowl though charming, is heavy and with dough in it even heavier. It holds and distributes heat well and *invites* the dough as no other bowl quite does. Stainless steel bowls that come in graduated sizes are light and easy to clean. Stainless steel conducts heat faster than ceramic. You needn't be too fussy. Anything that you have that's big enough will do.

**Measuring spoons**

For accurate measurements, spoons must be perfectly shaped without dents. Stainless steel spoons are preferable to plastic ones, in that the latter can absorb flavors and odors from other foods, possibly spreading them to the food being measured. For this reason plastic cookware in general is not recommended.

**Measuring cups**

Glass cups are for measuring liquid ingredients. Hold them at eye level for an accurate reading. Nested stainless steel cups are for exact dry measurements. A straight-edged knife or spatula can be used to level the top. Avoid aluminum, which reacts with certain acid foods and can impart a bitter taste to the food being measured. A wide variety of measuring cups, ranging from one-eighth-cup through six-cup capacity, can be very helpful.

**Rubber spatula**

Pliable rubber spatulas are a great help to the bread maker. For stirring, folding, creaming and scraping, if you like everything used to the very last drop, they are indispensable.

**Long-handled spoon or wooden spatula**

Long-handled wooden spoons with well-sanded bowls or wooden spatulas, whose flat surface is even more practical, are perfect tools for whipping your sponge. Wood is a warm material that, unlike metal, will not conduct heat. It is soft so it will not scratch surfaces and it will not discolor food or leave a metallic taste as metal sometimes does. Avoid aluminum spoons for the reasons stated on page 72. (See also Measuring Cups above.)

**Dough and other whisks**

A dough whisk is also a good utensil for whipping a sponge. Whisks in general are very efficient for beating eggs, for cooking easily overthickened cornmeal, and for creaming butter.

**Large towel**

You want a towel that is both big enough to cover generously the circumference of your large bowl and porous enough to absorb and hold moisture for several hours.

# For Kneading the Dough

**Kneading surface**

When kneading and working dough you want a certain amount of adhesion from your working surface. A bread baker to some extent depends on the ability of his surface to "grab" the dough, especially when he is shaping free-form loaves. A marble surface is wonderful because it provides a cool, nonporous, easily cleanable platform to which dough, even dough with a high fat content, will adhere but miraculously not stick (the coolness prevents precipitous softening). Wooden surfaces will "pull" the dough and their warm, natural quality is highly compatible with bread, though not as compatible with pastry or less glutenous doughs. Wooden surfaces, being porous, absorb odors and are sightly more difficult to clean, though some have been treated to resist moisture and bacteria. If you use a wooden cutting board, reserve it solely for bread and keep it spotless. You may anchor your wooden cutting board to the counter by placing a damp towel under it.

**Pastry scraper or dough knife**

A pastry scraper or dough knife (it functions as the latter when held perpendicularly) has a rectangular stainless steel

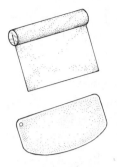

blade riveted to a wooden handle. It is a very useful tool for remassing dough while kneading and for cleaning stray particles of flour and dough from your work surface when you are through kneading. Choose one with a thin flexible blade for greater control and maneuverability. A U-shaped rubber version is excellent for working flour into doughs while they are still in the bowl and for cleaning the bowl itself afterwards.

# For Shaping the Dough

**Scale**

A kitchen scale or one that registers small increments of weight up to five pounds is helpful for bread makers in standardizing loaf sizes. Weighing ingredients is also much more accurate than measuring them, but Americans resist this and I have been discouraged from including measurements of weights. For bread making, a scale is not essential but, if you know exactly the size slice of bread you or your family likes for sandwiches, for example, you can more accurately repeat past performances by weighing the dough rather than eyeing it and estimating. For rolls and buns, a scale is a great help in avoiding an embarrassingly large or small product.

**Pans**

Pans of differing materials differ in their ability to absorb and conduct heat. As this will particularly affect the crust on the sides and bottom of your bread, it is important, in fashioning your perfect loaf, to choose the correct pan. If you are purchasing new equipment, select unmarred, sturdy, heavy-gauge pans. The heavier the metal, the more evenly baked the bread will be, and the pan itself will last longer. Do not spurn used equipment, to be found in flea markets, etc. Since pans temper with age, high-quality old equipment, still in good condition, can be preferable to new.

**Dark, dull-finished metals** Dark, dull-finished metals are wonderful for bread baking. They absorb heat well and will turn out bread with a thick, deep, golden-brown crust. Because they absorb rather than deflect heat, these materials are also more energy efficient.

**Aluminum** Though aluminum deflects heat and does not absorb it, it is an excellent heat conductor and is lightweight. The gauge or thickness of a particular aluminum determines its efficiency: the thicker and heavier the gauge, the more even the cooking. To prevent warps, dents, and uneven heating, aluminum should be at least one-eighth of an inch thick (or eight gauge). Some aluminum pans have not been electrochemically treated. This means that, not only will the pans discolor in contact with the minerals in water and foods, but also that highly acidic foods and those containing sulphur will be discolored and absorb a metallic taste. If you have untreated aluminum bread pans, line them with bakers' parchment before using.

**Teflon** Teflon is aluminum with a baked-on fluorocarbon resin that decreases its conductivity but gives it a nonstick surface. It will brown a crust but not quite so well as will dark, dull-finished metals. It tends to scratch easily. Since scratches destroy the nonstick finish, one should line scratched teflon pans with bakers' parchment. The fact that teflon does not require greasing is of benefit to those on low-fat diets. After baking it "releases" the bread easily.

**Pyrex or glass** Glass, which is a silicon (Pyrex is the brand name of a heat-proof glass) is a poor heat conductor, only slightly better than concrete, but, like dark, dull-finished metals, it radiates and transmits heat well. Convected oven heat begins to cook the contents of a glass pan from the top before conducted heat penetrates the glass at its sides and bottom. It is best, when using glass bakeware, to lower the oven temperature by 25°. Pyrex and glass are easy to clean and have the additional advantage of allowing you to view the dough as it gradually becomes bread.

**Earthenware** Earthenware is also a silicon and a poor heat conductor. Surprisingly, it is also a poor heat storer. It appears to hold heat because it is so slow to heat and slow to cool. As a result, earthenware, like an old-fashioned slackening oven, makes beautiful bread.

**Expandable loaf pan** The versatile expandable loaf pan makes a standard shaped loaf of bread but expands (either before or after you have poured in the dough) from nine to fifteen inches, allowing you to make different-sized breads without buying extra pans. Because the level to which the pan is filled has a direct effect on the appearance and texture of the finished bread, a pan that expands to your needs is a great convenience.

**Pullman pans** Often made of heavy-gauge black steel, pullman pans are rectangular with a removable, flat, sliding lid especially designed for sandwich bread (i.e., a close-grained bread with little crust). Another version, called a *pain de mie* pan, also of black steel, is long and cylindrical. This shape is designed for melba toast and cocktail breads.

Remember, in using a covered container, that the cover compacts the dough, making the bread denser. Since the fats in milk and butter soften the gluten and yield a particularly tender dough, some cooks choose to offset this density by using milk and butter doughs when baking in covered containers.

**La cloche**

A *cloche* is a large, unglazed, earthenware platter with a dome-shaped top. When put in an oven it becomes an oven within an oven. Inside the bell, which is an extremely efficient generator of moist heat, yeast grows quickly and the loaf is drawn up rather than spreading sideways as often happens with moist dough. A crust forms gradually, browns evenly and the crumb is able to grow to its full extent before the yeast is killed. This avoids a common failing—a crust formed so rapidly that it is overcooked and hard before the crumb has had a chance to expand properly.

A *cloche* produces very successful bread. You can improvise your own by inverting a pottery mixing bowl over a pottery pie dish. Tin does not work: it does not breathe and creates a clammy loaf. The main disadvantage to using a *cloche* is that, unless you have a very large oven (or two ovens), it is only feasible to bake one loaf at a time. You can, however, put the remaining dough in standard loaf pans. Usually two or three of these will fit in an oven around the sides of the *cloche*. When buttering or oiling the *cloche*, do not neglect the inside of the dome.

**Other unglazed clay pots or casseroles**

A wonderful discovery is that the same unglazed clay pots that you may have been using for roasting and stewing (ideally of very porous, highly fired clay) can also be used for bread. The thin vapor of steam released by the pots while they are in the oven provides a gentle heat, perfect for a soft inside and chewy crust. Freely improvise with all your clay cookware. Just remember to soak tops and bottoms in water for about ten or fifteen minutes before baking. This permits the clay to absorb moisture.

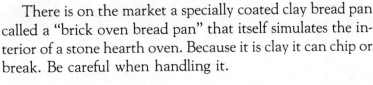

There is on the market a specially coated clay bread pan called a "brick oven bread pan" that itself simulates the interior of a stone hearth oven. Because it is clay it can chip or break. Be careful when handling it.

**Flower pots** Terracotta flower pots make terrific bread molds but there are a few tricks to using them. Purchase ones that have been "heated-tested." They may cost more, but they will not crack in the oven. Do not worry about a hole in the bottom. Dough will not leak through. Season the pots by coating them liberally inside and out with vegetable oil and leaving them, empty, in a fairly hot oven while something else is baking. Do this several times. Once they are impregnated with oil, they will need little greasing and loaves will easily slip out.

Bake the loaves upside down. The reason for this is that, when the dough is under a pot during the first few minutes of baking, it will spring up and fill the pot, creating an even and well-formed loaf. If the pot is upright, the dough is likely to balloon over, topple, and stick to the outside. First, fill your pots just over half full with dough. Stand them upright in a warm place to rise, covering the dough with a damp cloth. When the dough is within an inch and a half of the top, invert the pots onto a baking sheet and put them immediately into the oven. During the last ten or fifteen minutes of baking, remove the loaves from their pots, lower the temperature if necessary, and let them brown on all sides.

Cool the loaves on a rack or across the empty flower pots.

**Kugelhopf and bundt pans**

Kugelhopf and bundt pans fall into the general category of tube pans or baking pans with central holes. The tube conducts heat directly through the center of the dough so that a larger surface area of the dough or batter is exposed to concentrated heat. When a tube pan is called for, it is important either to use one or to divide the batter into several regular pans, thereby creating more than one surface. Savarin pans have a wide central hole. Kugelhopf and bundt pans have narrow central holes and are swirled and fluted on the sides.

**Charlotte mold**

A charlotte mold is a soufflé dish with slanted instead of straight sides. Charlotte molds are usually made of aluminum or tinned steel and the flared sides have ears (i.e., curved handles). Charlotte molds are usually used for dishes that have an outer layer, such as overlapping slices of thin bread encasing an inner filling, such as a fruit purée. After baking or jelling, the contents are inverted onto a serving platter.

**Brioche mold**

Brioche molds usually come in attractive materials such as tin, copper, or glazed pottery and in sizes that will accommodate individual rolls as well as three-cup and six-cup loaves. Scalloped flutings on the sides indent the dough and provide a greater heat conducting surface. Squat flared sides also permit the rising brioche to spread generously.

**Casseroles and baking dishes**

A casserole is a heat resistant dish with deep sides. A baking dish is a heat-resistant dish with shallow sides. Both should be heavy bottomed and made of a material that will absorb and hold heat. Copper, heavy enameled cast iron, and earthenware, particularly the kind that is glazed on the inside and unglazed on the outside (for greater heat absorption), are all good.

**Bain marie**

A *bain marie* (or water bath) consists of a vessel half-filled with hot (not boiling) water into which a second dish containing a food that is either to be baked or kept warm is placed. The entire ensemble is then put in the oven. Although water is a poor conductor of heat, it has a high capacity for heat storage. The combination is perfect when slow oven cooking is desirable.

**Corn stick pans**

Special pans for corn sticks are made of heavy, dark, cast iron. They must be seasoned before use (i.e., greased and baked empty) and, though expensive, make beautifully decorated miniature corn-on-the-cobs.

**Muffin tins**

Muffin tins come in 6-, 12-, and 24- cup sizes. Choose those that will fit on a single oven shelf. The cups should be seamless. Grease them well and fill them no more than two-thirds full for easy release after baking. Fill unused cups with water.

**Gem pans**

Gem pans are tins for miniature muffins.

**Bundt muffin pans**

Bundt muffin pans come in a tray like muffin pans but each cup is a miniature bundt-shaped mold with a cone in the center and swirled, fluted sides. The cone conducts heat to the center of the batter, which might otherwise remain uncooked. They make lovely festive muffins.

**Skillets**

Cast-iron skillets with cast-iron handles, which can go into the oven, are best for skillet breads. Cast iron browns nicely and releases nicely and is an excellent storer of heat. One variety comes divided into sections. This develops a crust on the sides of each individual piece.

**Baking and cookie sheets**

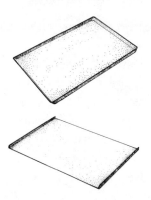

Because there is confusion about the difference between baking sheets and cookie sheets, I offer the following distinction. Baking sheets and jelly-roll pans are the same thing. They usually measure eleven-by-seventeen inches or twelve-by-eighteeen inches and have a small side rim. They are ideal for baking rounded loaves or breads in the shape of wreaths or braids and are perfect for biscuits. Cookie sheets are flat and rimless. When baking cookies it is important to use a cookie sheet because the oven's heat will pass over the top of the edge of a rimmed pan and will steam the cookie before baking it. The cookies also will tend to burn on the bottom before the top is thoroughly done.

# For Slitting and Glazing

**Sharp knife or razor**

Any small knife or razor with a sharp edge will do for slitting dough to ventilate the loaves before they go into the oven. The edge needs to be sharp as you must be able to control the depth of your slit. Because the response of a dull edge is more difficult to gauge, the risk of producing slits that may be too shallow or too deep is greater. (For more information about slitting, see page 56.)

**Pastry brushes**

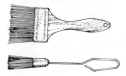

Have two, one for oiling pans and one for glazing loaves. Choose those with soft, flexible bristles (i.e., natural bristles) and clean them thoroughly after each use. Label them and reserve each one for its designated purpose.

# For Baking and Cooling

**Ovens**

The recipes in this book were tested in ordinary gas or electric home ovens. A convection oven, which cooks faster and browns more evenly (because a fan, housed in front of the heating element, continually circulates air through the oven) would be ideal. If you would like to adapt the recipes in this book to a convection oven, decrease the suggested oven temperature by 50°F and the baking time by a quarter or a third. Microwave ovens are not suitable for these recipes.

**Thermometers**

Have two permanently in your oven and move them from place to place occasionally. Each time you bake, compare them with each other and with the reading on your oven knob. As a baker it is essential that you are responsive to your oven's cold and hot spots. To prevent possible error, periodically have your oven calibrated so that the knobs reflect the oven's temperature as accurately as possible.

**Quarry tiles**

When placed side by side on a lower oven rack, quarry tiles, which are simply five and a half-inch squares of unglazed clay, simulate the baking conditions of an old style European clay oven. They provide very even heat distribution and, when hearth loaves are placed directly on them, as is desirable, more of the dough is exposed to the oven's heat. During baking, the porous clay also absorbs moisture from the bottom of the loaf, producing a thick, crusty crust. Stone baking is particularly suitable for the less refined peasant-style breads.

It is also possible to line a bottom oven shelf with quarry tiles and bake loaves in regular loaf pans placed either on the stones or on a middle or upper shelf. Though not reaping the full advantage of the tiles, the bread still benefits from the more evenly diffused oven heat.

**Baking stone**

Instead of a number of smaller tiles, you can buy a large, fourteen- or sixteen-inch, circular or rectangular tile known as a *baking stone*. Baking stones provide a half-inch thick baking surface on a half-inch raised platform that has channels molded into it to allow heat to circulate freely. Dry heat rises from the stone during baking and creates a deep rich crust. Place the stone in the oven on the lowest shelf on which you will be baking, dust it with a small sprinkling of cornmeal and bake on it directly. Before using the stone for the first time, you must season it by washing it in warm water and baking it at 450°F for thirty minutes. This conditions and hardens the stone, improving its baking properties. Be mindful. The stone is durable but can break or chip if dropped.

**Cooling racks**

As soon as loaves are removed from the oven, they must be ventilated. Cooling racks allow steam to evaporate evenly from all surfaces. You can improvise a cooling rack with an oven rack if the crossbars are fairly close together, or you can straddle a loaf over two loaf pans. Commercial wooden or wire cooling racks are slightly easier to use. Since wood does not conduct heat, it is the perfect material. (Rub with oil before using.) Choose sturdy racks with nearly adjacent crossbars (spaced between a quarter and half an inch apart), so that the rungs will not leave depressions in your bread and so that the same cooling rack will also serve for cooling delicate cakes and pastries. Because it raises the loaf and allows air to circulate around it evenly, a cooling rack is also perfect for defrosting bread.

# Other Useful Equipment

**Citrus peeler**

A citrus peeler is a tiny device from which citrus peel is shed in four thin worms. It is easy to use and wash. Your knuckles remain intact, and the peels are entirely accessible instead of clinging to a remote inner corner as they often do in the usual grater.

**Grinders for spices**

Freshly ground spices are preferable to prepackaged ones. Whenever possible purchase your spices whole and grind them just before using. Clean the grinder thoroughly before grinding a second, different spice. An ordinary pepper grinder can be used to grind spices that are approximately the size of a peppercorn. An electric coffee mill may be reserved for spices only. Spices can also be ground in a mortar and pestle, a blender, a food processor, and old-fashioned hand-operated coffee grinder, or by being placed between two sheets of wax paper and crushed with a bottle or rolling pin. For nutmeg, there are many gadgets on the market. A very good one, which shaves the nutmeg instead of grinding it, is called a *nut twister.* Avoid mass-marketed, cheap, tiny graters. The cutting edges on them are stamped out and do not cut well.

**Ice-cream scoops**

Ice-cream scoops, particularly the kind whose contents are released by a lever pressed by the thumb, are perfect for transferring muffin batter from the mixing bowl to the muffin cup.

**Serrated knife**

A serrated knife is ideal for foods such as bread that are hard on the outside and soft on the inside. The best kind has a ground, instead of stamped, blade of high carbon stainless steel. Pure carbon rusts, is soft, and stains easily. All stainless is very hard so that it is difficult to keep a sharp blade. The combination of both makes a perfect knife. Use it only for breads. *Never* put your serrated knife in the dishwasher. Handwash it in hot soapy water and then immediately dry it thoroughly. Store in a slotted or magnetic rack.

# Cleaning after Baking

**Metal pastry scraper**

The aforementioned flat-edged metal pastry scraper is ideal for cleaning flour and dough from your kneading surface. Use it first and then go over everything with a wet rag. Sponges are not practical for this purpose because flour tends to clog the sponge's pores, destroying its cleaning and absorbing qualities.

**Rubber pastry scraper**

The rubber U-shaped pastry scraper is a perfect tool for scraping off the dough stuck to your bread bowl before washing it.

**Long-handled brushes**

Long-handled wooden brushes that are so useful for washing dishes will not do for bread dough. The dough tends to work its way up between the bristles as well as sticking to the ends of them.

**Scouring pads**

Scouring pads reserved especially for bread-making equipment are a courtesy that everyone in your family will appreciate. Dough tends to stick tenaciously to the very pads that do the best job of getting it off your utensils. If you do not isolate them, or discard them frequently, you will be forever having little flecks of bread dough all over your other dishes.

**Do not wash bread pans**

Try never to wash your bread pans. Merely wipe them clean to preserve the seasoning that helps the bread to bake faster and not to stick. If you must wash them, do not use abrasives, especially on nonstick surfaces. And remember, any pan other than those made from stainless steel will rust if not dried thoroughly. Pans with rolled edges tend to collect water under the rolls. Be careful. Try putting your freshly washed pans back in the oven and be sure all the moisture has evaporated. Out of respect for the pans, store them neatly.

**Clean your oven**

A clean oven will get hotter than a dirty one and will also heat up more quickly. Both variables will markedly affect baking time and the texture of your crust.

**Oil wooden surfaces**

Oil any wooden surface that you use for kneading regularly with cooking oil. It will help prevent the dough from sticking and preserve the wood.

# Part IV

# THE SPONGE
# METHOD

# THE SPONGE
# METHOD

**What is a
sponge?**

A sponge is basically a batter made by whipping air into a combination of yeast, liquid, and about a third of the total amount of flour. This mixture is prepared and allowed to rise before the rest of the ingredients are added and the dough kneaded. Yeast, in the absence of inhibitors such as salt, shortening, and any of the heavier ingredients and in the presence of a lot of oxygen, grows quickly, giving the dough a good stretch. Gluten is formed while the sponge stretches. You don't have to do anything.

It is easier to incorporate the remaining ingredients into this elastic frothy mixture than to mix all of the ingredients together at the outset. A sponge also makes the mixture easier to knead. The grain of the flour gets more time to soften and the gluten more time to ripen. The difference in the texture and taste of the bread will more than compensate for the extra step.

**Proper
consistency**

A sponge can vary in consistency from a viscous batter to a thin syrup, depending on the time it will be given to ferment. Since the activity of a sponge can happen faster in a thinner medium, the shorter the time you have to give your sponge, the more fluid it should be. Yeast multiplies readily in a liquid medium where the food supply is mobile and where the yeast itself, also mobile, can continually seek out new sources of food. When the medium is too thick (dough being the extreme), the motility of the yeast is inhibited and if the sustenance within reach of the yeast is exhausted, which will happen unless it is manually redistributed, either by kneading or punching down, the yeast is likely to starve or suffocate in its own waste products. If a sponge has too little flour, however, the main activity that will take place during sponge time is yeast reproduction. This is valuable but not as valuable as the fermenting of the flour. The perfect condition is that of a thickish batter that has sufficient flour to be fermented by the yeast and other organisms but still fluid enough for the ecosystem to maintain itself. The benefits of a thicker sponge will increase the longer it is allowed to stand.

**Sponge and straight doughs**

Even a short-process sponge is preferable to a short-process straight dough. Because a sponge dough matures more quickly, a sponge process can produce better bread faster than any other method will, so, even if you have only a short time to give your bread, it is still better to use the sponge method.

**Time is incremental**

Baking bread is not an endeavor that requires your attention the whole day. Nevertheless, you need to be able to return to the same place (your kitchen), even if just for a few minutes, at several stages. Lapses between visits can be as long as a day or even two days, so the bond is not as commanding as is commonly assumed. Nevertheless, do not try to save time making yeasted breads. If you want to save time or spend only a short time making bread, select a method more appropriate. Quick breads, for example, which rise fast and require no kneading, are designed expressly for this purpose. (See pages 144–94) for recipes.)

**How to use the five-step procedure**

Remember that the sponge method is merely a technique for bread making and that any recipe may be adapted to its principles (see page 88 for the alterations to a conventional recipe for egg bread that has been adapted to the sponge method). The yeasted bread recipes included in this book are laid out according to the five steps involved in the sponge method. If you first familiarize yourself with the following description of how to do each step and with the preceding discussion of the methods and principles involved, you will find, when you turn to the recipes themselves, it a simple matter to adapt the appropriate ingredients.

**If you don't use a sponge**

Beneficial though a sponge may be, all breads can be made without one. You can compensate for the lack of a sponge to some extent by kneading extra long and carefully and by allowing the dough to rise as gradually as possible. It is especially important without a sponge to punch the dough down and to let it rise several times. The idea is to stretch the glutenous fibers. You *can* do with your muscles and several extended rising periods what the sponge does for you. It is just harder and less certain.

# PROCEDURE FOR THE SPONGE METHOD

Try to gather all of the equipment and ingredients that you will need for the whole recipe at the beginning so that they will be at hand and at room temperature.

The recipe in the following description is for a whole-wheat bread. However, the procedure is applicable to any bread recipe. The recipes in this book have been designed for the sponge method, but the sponge itself may be omitted: simply combine all the ingredients from both Steps I and II, do not whip the mixture, and continue according to the directions for Step II.

## EQUIPMENT AND INGREDIENTS

**Large bowl**

**Measuring spoons and cup**

**Rubber spatula**

**Long-handled spoon or wire whisk**

**Large towel or plastic wrap**

**1/4 cup honey**

**2-1/2 cups milk, scalded and cooled to lukewarm**

**1 tablespoon active dry yeast**

**1/2 cup brewers' yeast** *(optional)*

**2 cups unbleached white bread flour**

**2 cups whole-wheat flour**

## STEP I
## Preparing the Sponge

If you are using a sweetener, measure it into the large bowl first. Heat the liquid or cool the scalded milk to lukewarm (between 100° and 105°F) or, if you are using tap water, run the water until it is very hot. Put the correct amount of liquid into the same measurer that you used for the sweetener to dissolve any that remains. Then pour the liquid into the large bowl. This transfer of hot water to two separate surfaces cools it down to just the proper degree. (If you choose to add eggs to a recipe, break them into a measuring cup and be sure to reduce the liquid called for by the quantity of egg you are adding.)

Add the yeast, the brewers' yeast, if desired, and enough of the high-gluten flour you are using to make a batter that can be whipped with a whisk or long-handled spoon. Because of the particular technique involved, an electric mixer cannot be used to whip a sponge. To avoid adding too much flour, add it gradually, a cup or so at a time, and beat it well with small up and down strokes after each addition. You will end up with a mixture quite thick but still easy to beat. Then whip for a hundred strokes, dipping your whisk or spoon just under the top surface. Count each stroke. (The idea is to whip in lots of air.) Your finished sponge will look puffed and billowy. Cover the bowl with a warm, damp towel or sheet of plastic pulled tightly across the top, so that the sponge does not lose moisture, and let it rest as long as you can. Between forty-five minutes and two hours is adequate (this is called a *flying sponge*), but any time from fifteen minutes to eight hours is acceptable. After this the yeast exhausts itself.

## STEP II
# Kneading and Rising

**Lightly floured kneading surface**

**1/4 cup unsalted butter, softened**

**1 cup wheat germ**

**3/4 to 1-3/4 cup unbleached white bread flour**

**1 cup whole-wheat flour**

From this point on, you should be aware of your dough as a unity. You do not want to tear it, or cut into it, or do anything that will lessen its strength and elasticity. To incorporate the remaining ingredients therefore, you must *fold them in*, sprinkling or pouring them into the center of the sponge and folding the batter over from the outer edges.

Add the salt, shortening (embellishments may be added now or in Step IV), and *most* of the rest of the flour. Reserve some for the kneading. Gradually fold these ingredients in until the dough holds together and begins to come cleanly off the sides of the bowl. Dump the contents, which will appear somewhat ragged and limp, onto your kneading surface. The stray flour from the bowl will probably be enough to begin with. Scrape it out and incorporate it little by little.

Flour your hands and begin kneading until the dough feels "springy and alive" (the consistency of your ear-lobe) and the holes made by pressing two fingers into it vanish. Add flour gradually in small amounts. Less and less flour will be necessary and eventually no flour at all will be needed to prevent the dough from sticking. Before you finish, scrape the kneading surface and add the scrapings to your mound of dough. If you wish, clean your bowl, but it is not essential, and butter or oil it. Place the dough in it. Then turn the dough over, being sure that the entire surface is thoroughly greased. Cover the bowl again with a warm damp cloth and let the dough rest until it has approximately doubled in size. Since each environment differs, it is difficult to estimate how long this will take. Two hours is perhaps average.

When it has risen sufficiently, punch the dough down, using firm, hard strokes so that all the air is expelled. Then let it rise again. The dough will double in volume in about two-thirds of the time of the previous rising. Again test for readiness by pressing two fingers into the dough. If the holes remain, it has stretched all it can and is ready to be shaped.

## STEP III
# Cutting and Shaping

**Loaf pan or metal sheet**
**Brush for oiling**
**Kitchen scale for weighing** *(optional)*

Punch the dough down again. Remove the dough from its bowl, knead it a little to release all the air and let it rest for five minutes so that the gluten relaxes. Then divide, or weigh the dough into the desired amounts for loaves and let the mounds of dough rest again. Now that you know the exact quantity of your dough, choose your pans and oil them with a brush reserved for this purpose. Shape the loaves by kneading each mound briefly until the dough is compact, adding embellishments if you have waited until now, and easing the dough into a log, which you turn into the pan seam-side up. Press the dough firmly into the corners and floor of the pan. Then turn it upside-down so that the dough falls into your hand and replace it, seam-side down. Cover the pan with a damp cloth to prevent a skin from forming on the loaf and let the bread rise until the center of the loaf becomes level with the top edge of the pan. *Do not let it over rise.* Meanwhile preheat the oven and, if using them, prepare the glaze and seeds for topping.

## STEP IV
# Slitting and Glazing

**Sharp knife or razor**
**Glazing brush**

*Glaze:* **1 egg + 1 teaspoon water**

Using a sharp knife or razor, slash the top of the bread decoratively with shallow slits. (See pages 56–60 for design suggestions.) Brush the loaves with a glaze (see page 61 for variations) and sprinkle on the seeds. Place the pans in a preheated oven, allowing as much air and heat to circulate around the pans as possible.

## STEP V
# Baking and Cooling

**Cooling racks**
**Packaging material**
*(optional)*

Bake your bread at 350°F for between thirty-five and fifty minutes, or until the loaves test done (see page 64). You may want to change shelves or shelf position half-way through. You may want to remove the loaves from their pans for the last five or eight minutes, use a higher temperature for the first ten minutes, or spray the loaves with water for a hard crust.

When the bottom of your loaves sound hollow to your tap, the sides are firm, and the color is deep and golden, remove the loaves to cooling racks. Study their appearance and memorize every quality so that you will learn to recognize a perfectly baked loaf. For certain effects you may want to glaze the hot loaves immediately, but do not package the bread until it has cooled thoroughly. This will take about three hours.

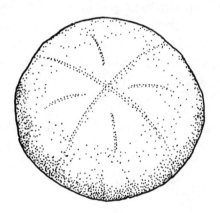

To show how any bread dough may be adapted to the sponge method, here is a recipe set out in the traditional manner and then translated, as it were, to the sponge method.

---

*Traditional Recipe:*
# Country Fair Egg Bread

| | |
|---|---|
| 1-1/2 cups scalded milk | 2 cakes yeast |
| 1/2 cup butter | 1/2 cup lukewarm water |
| 2 teaspoons salt | 2 eggs, beaten |
| 1/2 cup sugar | About 9 cups flour, sifted |

Pour the scalded milk over the butter, salt, and sugar. Cool. Dissolve the yeast in the lukewarm water and let stand until it bubbles, about 5 minutes. Add the yeast and the beaten eggs to the cooled milk. Gradually add the flour, beating it in thoroughly. Do not add any more flour than is necessary to make an easily handled dough, as the bread should be light and tender. Turn out onto floured board and knead until smooth and elastic. Place in greased bowl, cover, and let rise until doubled in size, about 1½ hours. Punch down and turn out onto a lightly floured board. Shape into 3 loaves and place in greased 8-inch loaf pans. Cover and let rise until dough is just to the tops of the pans. Bake in a 425° oven for 10 minutes, then lower heat to 350° and bake 40 minutes longer, or until bread is done. Makes 3 loaves.

From Dolores Casella, *A World of Breads* (Port Washington, N.Y.: David White, 1966), pp. 54–55.

## Adaptation to the Sponge Method

STEP I.  1-1/2 cups scalded milk, cooled to lukewarm
1/2 cup lukewarm water
1/2 cup sugar
1 cake yeast *or* 1 package (i.e., 1 tablespoon) active dry yeast
3 to 4 cups flour *(see below)*

Combine all of the liquid in the recipe. You will use the same amount but because you will add the yeast directly to it, cool it to lukewarm first. Use only 1 cake, or one package, of yeast. The original recipe has two in order to speed up the rising process. Dissolve the yeast and sugar in the lukewarm liquid. Then add enough of the flour to make a batter that can be whipped with a wire whisk (see the directions on page 84). Let the sponge rise (see the instructions on page 85).

*STEP II.*     **2 teaspoons salt**
**1/2 cup butter**
**2 eggs, at room temperature, beaten**
**5 to 6 cups flour, about 9 cups total** *(see below)*

To the risen sponge add the salt, butter, which should be at room temperature, the beaten eggs, and enough of the remaining flour so that the dough begins to hold together and come cleanly away from the sides of the bowl. Turn the mass out onto a kneading surface and knead according to the instructions on p. 85, adding flour as necessary for the desired consistency. The total amount of flour used in Steps I and II should be the 9 cups called for in the original recipe. The sponge method does not require *more* flour; the total amount is simply added in stages.

*STEPS III to V.*     **Follow the original recipe.**

As you can see, the difficulties in transcribing an ordinary bread recipe to the sponge method lie mainly in recognizing the order in which the ingredients should be incorporated into the dough so as not to hamper the growth of the yeast or the development of gluten, and in determining how much flour should be added in Step I and how much in Step II. The order of ingredients follows a formula and requires only a basic knowledge of the bread-making process. An understanding of how to add flour to develop a dough also comes after not very many experiments with making a sponge and kneading dough to the correct consistency. If you are a beginner or new to the sponge method, choose one simple bread from the Yeasted Bread section of this book. Make it several times until you are satisfied that you understand each step in the procedure. At that point, *any* recipe in *any* book will readily lend itself to the sponge method.

# Part V

# RECIPES

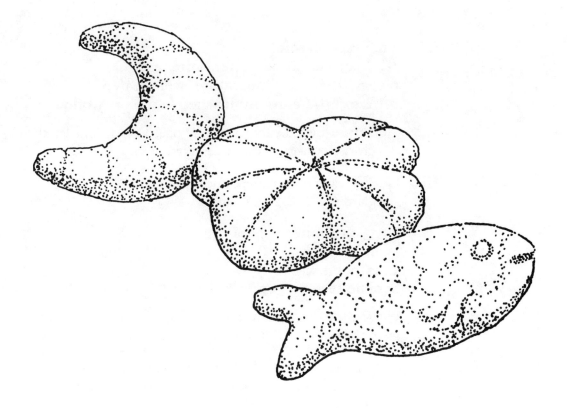

*The yeasted recipes from page 92 to page 141 use the five-step
sponge method. Please refer back to the Sponge Method section,
page 82 to page 87, as needed.*

Makes three 4½-by-8½-inch loaves

## Egg Bread

*Almost cake. The cheese version is one of my very favorite breads.*

STEP I.    **1/4 to 1/2 cup honey**
**2 cups milk, scalded and cooled to lukewarm**
**1 tablespoon active dry yeast**
**3 cups unbleached white bread flour**

Prepare the sponge. Allow it to rise from 45 minutes to 2 hours.

STEP II.   **1 tablespoon salt**
**1-1/2 cups unsalted butter, softened**
**6 eggs, at room temperature, well beaten**
**5-1/2 to 6-1/2 cups unbleached white bread flour**

Add these ingredients to the sponge, knead, and let the dough rise at least once, preferably twice.

STEP III.  Cut the dough and shape the loaf-sized pieces to fit three standard 4½-by-8½-inch pans.

STEP IV.   **1 egg, at room temperature**
 ***mixed with***
**1 teaspoon water**
**Sesame seed or poppyseed**

Slit the top of the loaves with a razor or sharp knife and glaze them. Sprinkle the top with the seeds.

STEP V.    Bake the loaves in a 350°F oven for 35 to 40 minutes or until they test done. Transfer the loaves to a cooling rack to cool completely.

VARIATIONS Embellishments may be added just before the dough is shaped into loaves.

*Raisin bread:* Knead in 1¼ cup raisins per loaf.

*Cheese bread:* Knead in 1¼ cup grated Parmesan or Asiago cheese per loaf.

# Semolina Bread

*Finely ground flour from the sweet part of the wheat
infuses this creamy loaf with a delicate cornlike flavor.*

STEP I.

1/2 cup honey
3 cups lukewarm water
1 tablespoon active dry yeast
1/2 cup powdered milk
3 to 5 cups semolina flour

Prepare the sponge. Allow it to rise from 45 minutes to 2
hours.

STEP II.

2 teaspoons salt
1/2 cup corn oil
3-3/4 to 4-3/4 cups semolina flour

Add these ingredients to the sponge, knead, and let the
dough rise at least once, preferably twice.

STEP III.

Cut the dough and shape the loaf-sized pieces into 3 standard 4½-by-8½-inch loaves.

STEP IV.

1 egg, at room temperature
*mixed with*
1 teaspoon milk
Cornmeal

Slit the top of the loaves with a razor or sharp knife and
glaze them. Dust lightly with cornmeal.

STEP V.

Bake the loaves in a 350°F oven for 35 to 45 minutes or
until they test done. Transfer them to a cooling rack to cool
completely.

Makes four 1½-pound, three 2-pound, or six 1-pound loaves

# Potato Bread

*Here is an egg bread with morsels of potato and slivers of potato skin.*

STEP I.
1/2 cup honey
1-1/2 cups lukewarm potato water
1 tablespoon active dry yeast
2 cups unbleached white bread flour

Prepare the sponge. Allow it to rise from 45 minutes to 2 hours.

STEP II.
1 tablespoon salt
1/2 cup unsalted butter, softened
6 eggs, at room temperature, well beaten
3 cups cooked, unpeeled potatoes mashed with butter and milk; leave small pieces for taste and appearance
1 cup potato flour
6 to 7 cups unbleached white bread flour

Add these ingredients to the sponge, knead, and let the dough rise at least once, preferably twice.

STEP III.
Cut the dough and shape the loaf-sized pieces. One-pound loaves made in little one-pound loaf pans are particularly attractive with this dough. Bake them for a shorter time.

STEP IV.
1 egg, at room temperature
*mixed with*
1 teaspoon milk
Sesame seed or poppyseed for sprinkling on top

Slit the top of the loaves with a razor or sharp knife and glaze them. Sprinkle the tops with seeds.

STEP V.
Bake the loaves in a 350°F oven for 40 to 45 minutes or until they test done. Transfer the loaves to a cooling rack to cool completely.

# Fougasse

*A fougasse is a flat, irregularly shaped loaf made from plain, unsweetened dough. It is an imaginative bread to make and fun for guests to tug off odd-sized portions.*

STEP I.
**2 tablespoons yeast**
**2-1/2 cups lukewarm water**
**2-1/4 cups unbleached white bread flour**

Prepare the sponge. Allow it to rise from 45 minutes to 2 hours.

STEP II.
**2 teaspooons salt dissolved in 2 teaspoons water**
**4 to 5 cups unbleached white bread flour**

Add these ingredients to the sponge, knead, and let the dough rise at least once, preferably twice.

STEP III.
Divide the dough into four ¾-pound balls. Cover and let them rise for approximately 20 minutes, or until there is enough air that the dough can be punched down, then flattened, tossed, turned, and pulled until it is the size you want.

STEP IV.
**Olive oil** *or* **a glaze made from 1 egg, at room temperature, and 1 teaspoon water**
**Sesame seed** *(optional)*

Slash the loaves with a sharp razor, making sure that the dough is still thick enough to hold together. Brush with olive oil or egg glaze. The final rising will be very fast.

STEP V.
Bake the fougasse at 400°F for 10 minutes. Reduce the heat to 350°F and bake for an additional 30 minutes, or until the loaves test done. During baking, spray the bread and the whole oven with water once every 10 minutes until the crust is set. Cool the fougasse thoroughly on cooling racks.

VARIATIONS
*Walnut fougasse*
**2 tablespoons walnut oil**
**1 cup chopped walnuts**

Brush the top of the fougasse with oil and then sprinkle it with chopped walnuts.

*Olive fougasse*

**1 tablespoon olive oil**
**1 cup chopped pitted black olives, preferably**
   **Niçoise or meaty, Greek brine-cured olives**

Substitute white wine for part or all of the liquid. Brush the top of the fougasse with olive oil and then sprinkle it with the chopped olives.

*Herb fougasse*

**2 tablespoons olive oil**
**1/2 cup chopped fresh herbs, such as sage,**
   **marjoram, etc.**

Brush the top of the fougasse with olive oil and then sprinkle it with the chopped herbs.

---

Makes two 1½-pound loaves, not counting the filling

# Spiral Herb Bread

*The flavor of herbs is keen in this striking green and white pinwheel.*

STEP I.    **1 tablespoon active dry yeast**
           **1 cup scalded milk, cooled to lukewarm**
           **1 cup lukewarm water**
           **1-3/4 cups unbleached white bread flour**

Prepare the sponge. Allow it to rise from 45 minutes to 2 hours.

STEP II.   **2-1/2 teaspoons salt**
           **1/4 cup olive oil**
           **2 to 3 cups unbleached white bread flour**

Add these ingredients to the sponge, knead, and let the dough rise at least once, preferably twice.

**STEP III.**     *Herb filling*

**2 cups finely chopped fresh parsley**
**2 cups finely chopped scallions**
**1 clove garlic, minced**
**2 tablespoons unsalted butter**
**2 eggs, at room temperature, lightly beaten**
**1 teaspoon salt**
**Freshly ground pepper**
**Several drops of Tabasco sauce**

Cook the parsley, scallions, and garlic in butter until they are reduced to half their original volume. Cool. Reserve 2 tablespoons of the beaten eggs and add the rest to the vegetables and season them with salt, pepper, and Tabasco sauce. Divide the dough in half and shape each half into a ball. Roll each ball in a 6½-by-10-inch rectangle that is approximately ⅓ of an inch thick. Brush the rectangles with the reserved egg and spread the filling to within 1 inch of the edges. Roll them jelly-roll fashion, slice off the ends without filling and place the breads in greased 9-by-5-by-3-inch bread pans, seam side down.

**STEP IV.**     **Melted butter**

Do not slit the loaves. Brush the tops with melted butter.

**STEP V.**     Bake the loaves in a 400°F oven for 10 minutes. Lower the temperature to 350°F and continue baking until the loaves test done. Transfer them to a cooling rack to cool completely.

Makes two standard
4½-by-8½-inch loaves

## Whole-Wheat Bread

*A light, unadorned whole wheat.*

**STEP I.**
1/4 cup honey
2-1/2 cups milk, scalded and cooled to lukewarm
1 tablespoon active dry yeast
1/2 cup brewers' yeast (*optional*)
2 cups unbleached white bread flour
2 cups whole-wheat flour *or* proportion flours to
   taste, using a total of 4 cups

Prepare the sponge. Allow it to rise from 45 minutes to 2 hours.

**STEP II.**
1 tablespoon salt
1/4 cup unsalted butter, softened
1 cup wheat germ
3/4 to 1-3/4 cups unbleached white bread flour
1 cup whole-wheat flour *or* proportion flours to
   taste, using a total of 1-3/4 to 2-3/4 cups

Add these ingredients to the sponge, knead, and let the dough rise at least once, preferably twice.

**STEP III.**
Cut the dough and shape the loaf-sized pieces into 2 standard 4½-by-8½-inch loaves.

**STEP IV.**
1 egg, at room temperature
   *mixed with*
1 teaspoon water
**Sesame seed for topping**

Slit the top of the loaves with a razor or sharp knife and glaze them. Sprinkle the tops with seeds.

**STEP V.**
Bake the loaves in a 350°F oven for 35 to 40 minutes or until they test done. You may remove the loaves from their baking pans 10 minutes early to brown further. Cool the loaves thoroughly on cooling racks.

Makes two 1¾-pound
loaves and one 1-pound
round

# Whole-Wheat Molasses Bread

*A sweet, melt-in-your-mouth molasses taste and chewy texture.*

STEP I.

**3/4 cup unsulphured molasses**
**1 cup lukewarm water**
**1 cup lukewarm milk**
**1/4 teaspoon ginger**
**4 teaspoons active dry yeast**
**1-1/2 cups whole-wheat pastry flour**
**2-1/2 cups whole-wheat flour**

Prepare the sponge. Allow it to rise from 45 minutes to 2 hours.

STEP II.

**1 tablespoon salt**
**1/2 cup unsalted butter, melted**
**2 eggs, at room temperature**
**1 cup bran**
**2-1/3 cups whole-wheat pastry flour**
**1 to 1-2/3 cups whole-wheat flour**

Add these ingredients to the sponge, knead, and let the dough rise at least once, preferably twice.

STEP III.

Shape dough into round loaves (an especially nice shape for this bread).

STEP IV.

**Melted butter**

Slit the top of the loaves with a razor or sharp knife. Brush the dough with melted butter and reserve some of the butter.

STEP V.

**Reserved melted butter**

Bake the loaves in a 350°F oven for 35 to 40 minutes. Brush the loaves again with melted butter as soon as they are taken from the oven. Cool them thoroughly on cooling racks.

# Whole-Wheat Apple Bread

*An intensely flavored whole-grained bread with apple bits, apple juice, and apple butter; very nice with peanut butter.*

**STEP I.**
1/4 cup honey
2 cups apple juice, heated to lukewarm
1 tablespoon active dry yeast
1-1/2 cups whole-wheat flour
2 cups unbleached white bread flour *or* proportion
    flours to taste, using a total of 3-1/2 cups

Prepare the sponge. Allow it to rise from 45 minutes to 2 hours.

**STEP II.**
2 teaspoons salt
1/4 cup unsalted butter, softened
1/2 cup apple butter
1 cup dried apples, coarsely chopped
1-1/2 cups whole-wheat flour
2 to 3 cups unbleached white bread flour *or*
    proportion flours to taste, using a total of 3-1/2
    to 4-1/2 cups

Add these ingredients to the sponge, knead, and let the dough rise at least once, preferably twice.

**STEP III.**
Cut the dough and shape the loaf-sized pieces into 2 standard 4½-by-8½ inch loaves.

**STEP IV.**
1 egg, at room temperature
   *mixed with*
1 teaspoon water
Cornmeal

Slit the top of the loaves with a razor or sharp knife and glaze them. Dust lightly with cornmeal.

**STEP V.**
Bake the loaves in a 350°F oven for 35 to 40 minutes or until they test done. Transfer the loaves to cooling racks to cool completely.

Makes about two 1¾-pound loaves (which is a nice amount for this bread) and one 1-pound round

# Hazelnut Bread

*A distinctive bread subtly perfused with apples and spices.*

**STEP I.**

**2 tablespoons firmly packed brown sugar**
**3/4 cup apple juice, heated to lukewarm**
**1 tablespoon active dry yeast**
**1/4 teaspoon freshly ground nutmeg**
**3/4 teaspoon cinnamon**
**3/4 cup whole-wheat flour**

Prepare the sponge. Allow it to rise from 45 minutes to 2 hours.

**STEP II.**

**1 teaspoon salt**
**1 egg, at room temperature, lightly beaten**
**1 cup applesauce**
**1/4 cup hazelnut oil**
**3/4 cup coarsely chopped hazelnuts**
**3 to 4 cups unbleached white bread flour**

Add these ingredients to the sponge, knead, and let the dough rise at least once, preferably twice.

**STEP III.**

Cut the dough and shape the loaf-sized pieces into two 1¾-pound standard size loaves and one 1-pound round.

**STEP IV.**

**Hazelnut oil**

Slit the top of the loaves with a razor or sharp knife and glaze them with the hazelnut oil.

**STEP V.**

**Apple juice**

Bake the loaves in a 350°F oven for 40 to 45 minutes or until they test done. During baking, baste the loaves every 10 minutes or so with the apple juice. Transfer the loaves to cooling racks to cool completely.

Makes two 1½-pound
standard size loaves and
one 1¼-pound round

# Graham Bread

*A coarsely textured bread abundantly flecked with
graham wheat.*

STEP I.
1/4 cup firmly packed light brown sugar
1-1/2 cups lukewarm water
1 can (13 ounces) evaporated milk, heated to
  lukewarm
1 tablespoon active dry yeast
1-1/2 cups graham flour
1-1/2 unbleached white bread flour

Prepare the sponge. Allow it to rise from 45 minutes to 2
hours.

STEP II.
1 tablespoon salt
1/3 cup unsalted butter, softened
1-1/4 cups graham flour
1-1/2 to 2-1/2 cups unbleached white bread flour

Add these ingredients to the sponge, knead, and let the
dough rise at least once, preferably twice.

STEP III.
Cut the dough and shape the loaf-sized pieces into two
1½-pound standard sized loaves and one 1¼-pound round.

STEP IV.
**Milk**

Slit the top of the loaves with a razor or sharp knife and
glaze them with milk.

STEP V.
Bake the loaves in a 375°F oven for 35 to 40 minutes or until
they test done. Transfer the loaves to a cooling rack to cool
completely.

# Graham Bread with Alfalfa Sprouts

*With raisins and orange juice and sprouts we have a
nourishing miniature breakfast.*

Soak 2⅓ cups of raisins in ½ cup of orange juice while
preparing the dough.

**STEP I.**
**1/3 cup honey**
**3 cups lukewarm water**
**1 tablespoon active dry yeast**
**1 cup powdered milk**
**3 cups unbleached white bread flour**
**1-1/2 cups graham flour**

Prepare the sponge. Allow it to rise from 45 minutes to 2
hours.

**STEP II.**
**1 tablespoon salt**
**1/3 cup safflower oil**
**2 cups graham flour**
**1 cup roasted soy flour**
**2 cups alfalfa sprouts sprinkled with 2 teaspoons
  fresh lemon juice**
**The soaked raisins (do not drain)**
**3-1/2 to 4-1/2 cups unbleached white bread flour**

Add these ingredients to the sponge, knead, and let the
dough rise at least once, preferably twice. You may knead
the dough in two portions if you want to make it slightly
easier to handle.

**STEP III.**
Cut the dough and shape the loaf-sized pieces into three
standard 4½-by-8½-inch loaves.

**STEP IV.**
**1 egg, at room temperature**
  *mixed with*
**1 teaspoon water**
**Sesame seed for topping**

Slit the top of the loaves with a razor or sharp knife and
glaze them. Sprinkle the top with seeds.

**STEP V.**
Bake the loaves in a 350°F oven for 35 to 40 minutes or until
they test done. Transfer the loaves to cooling racks to cool
completely.

Makes three 1½-pound rounds

## Buttermilk Rye Bread

*The loveliest taste and aroma of orange.*

**STEP I.**
**1/2 cup unsulphured molasses *or* 1/4 cup molasses + 1/4 cup firmly packed light brown sugar**
**1 cup lukewarm water**
**1 tablespoon active dry yeast**
**2 cups buttermilk mixed with 2 eggs, lightly beaten, all at room temperature**
**1-1/4 cups rye flour**
**2 cups unbleached white bread flour**

Prepare the sponge. Allow it to rise from 45 minutes to 2 hours.

**STEP II.**
**1 tablespoon salt**
**1/4 cup unsalted butter, softened**
**2 tablespoons crushed fennel seed**
**2 tablespoons crushed caraway seed**
**1/2 teaspoon baking soda**
**Grated rind of 4 oranges**
**2 cups rye flour**
**1-3/4 to 2-3/4 cups unbleached white bread flour**

Add these ingredients to the sponge, knead, and let the dough rise at least once, preferably twice. The dough will be sticky. Do not be alarmed. Work quickly so as not to have to add too much flour while kneading.

**STEP III.**
Cut the dough and shape the loaf-sized pieces into rounded loaves.

**STEP IV.**
**1 egg, at room temperature**
    *mixed with*
**1 teaspoon water**

Slit the top of the loaves with a razor or sharp knife and glaze them.

**STEP V.**
Bake the loaves in a 400°F for 10 minutes, then at 350°F for 30 to 35 minutes, or until they test done. Cool them thoroughly on cooling racks.

Makes two 1¾-pound loaves

# Ginger Rye

*Ginger, coffee, cinnamon, and anise pervade this sharp, sweet loaf.*

STEP I.
**2 cups freshly brewed coffee, cooled to lukewarm
1/4 cup firmly packed brown sugar
1 tablespoon active dry yeast
2 cups unbleached white bread flour**

Prepare the sponge. Allow it to rise from 45 minutes to 2 hours.

STEP II.
**2 teaspoons salt
1/4 cup olive oil
1 tablespoon whole anise seeds, crushed
2/3 cup crystallized ginger, chopped into medium-
     sized pieces
1/2 teaspoon cinnamon
2/3 cup rye flour
1-1/2 to 2-1/2 cups unbleached white bread flour**

Add these ingredients to the sponge, knead, and let the dough rise at least once, preferably twice.

STEP III.
Cut the dough and shape the loaf-sized pieces into two rounds weighing approximately 1-1/2 to 1-3/4 pounds each.

STEP IV.
**Olive oil**

Slit the top of the loaves with a razor or sharp knife and glaze them with olive oil.

STEP V.
Bake the loaves in a 350°F oven for 45 to 50 minutes or until they test done. If you have baking tiles, use them for a harder, crisper crust. Transfer the loaves to a cooling rack to cool completely.

VARIATION
For a softer ginger flavor, substitute preserved ginger in heavy syrup for the crystallized ginger. Use:

**1/2 cup of preserved ginger chopped into small
     pieces
1/4 cup of the syrup
Increase the rye flour to 1-1/4 cups**

Makes approximately
two 2-pound standard
loaves or three 1¼- to
1½-pound rounds

# Rye-Walnut Bread

*The flavor of walnuts fully penetrates an otherwise delicate rye.*

**STEP I.**

**1/4 cup honey**
**1 cup lukewarm water**
**1 cup milk, scalded and cooled to lukewarm**
**1 tablespoon active dry yeast**
**1 cup whole-wheat flour**
**1 cup unbleached white bread flour**

Prepare the sponge. Allow it to rise from 45 minutes to 2 hours.

**STEP II.**

**2 teaspoons salt**
**1/3 cup walnut oil**
**1 cup coarsely chopped walnuts**
**1 cup rye flour**
**1 cup whole-wheat flour**
**2 to 3 cups unbleached white bread flour**

Add these ingredients to the sponge, knead, and let the dough rise at least once, preferably twice.

**STEP III.**

Cut the dough and shape the loaf-sized pieces into two standard 4½-by-8½-inch loaves or into three rounds, if you prefer.

**STEP IV.**

**Water for glaze**

Slit the top of the loaves with a razor or sharp knife and glaze them with water just before baking. Bake the loaves for 5 minutes and brush them again with water.

**STEP V.**

Bake the loaves in a 350°F oven for 35 to 40 minutes, or until they test done. Transfer the loaves to cooling racks to cool completely.

# Light Pumpernickel Bread

*Potatoes and cornmeal lend a satisfying mellowness.*

STEP I.

**1-1/2 cups cold water**
**3/4 cup yellow cornmeal**
**1-1/2 cups boiling water**

Combine the ingredients in a saucepan. Whisk them constantly over low heat for 2 minutes or until they have thickened. Cool the mixture to lukewarm and add it to the sponge with the flours.

**1/4 cup unsulphured molasses**
**1 tablespoon active dry yeast dissolved in 1/4 cup**
**    lukewarm water**
**1-1/2 cups pumpernickel flour**
**2 cups unbleached white bread flour**

Prepare the sponge. Allow to rise 45 minutes to 2 hours.

STEP II.

**1 tablespoon salt**
**1/4 cup corn oil**
**1 tablespoon caraway seed**
**2 cups mashed potatoes**
**2 cups pumpernickel flour**
**1-1/2 to 2-1/2 cups unbleached white bread flour**

Add these ingredients to the sponge, knead, and let the dough rise at least once, preferably twice. The dough will be sticky. You may need to add an additional ½ cup of white flour for kneading. Work quickly to avoid having to add more than this.

STEP III.

**Cornmeal** (*optional*)

Cut the dough and shape the loaf-sized pieces into rounded loaves. After they rise, invert them onto a greased baking sheet or one sprinkled with cornmeal.

STEP IV.

**1 egg, at room temperature**
**    *mixed with***
**1 teaspoon water**

Slit the top of the loaves with a razor or sharp knife and glaze them.

STEP V.

Bake the loaves in a 450°F oven for 10 minutes, then at 350°F for 30 to 35 minutes, or until they test done. Cool the loaves thoroughly on cooling racks.

# Russian Black Bread

*A somewhat dense peasant bread, dark and earthy.
Black breads were traditionally darkened with crumbs
made from darkly toasted dark breads.*

**STEP I.**

**1/3 cup unsulphured molasses**
**2 cups lukewarm water**
**1 tablespoon active dry yeast**
**1/8 cup cider vinegar**
**1 cup rye flour**
**1 cup unbleached white bread flour**

Prepare the sponge. Allow it to rise from 45 minutes to 2
hours.

**STEP II.**

**2 teaspoons salt**
**1/4 cup unsalted butter, softened**
**1 cup All-Bran or darkly toasted dark breadcrumbs**
**1/4 cup unsweetened cocoa, sifted**
**2 teaspoons instant espresso coffee powder**
**1 teaspoon fennel seed, crushed**
**1/2 cup rye flour**
**1-1/2 to 2-1/2 cups unbleached white bread flour**

Add these ingredients to the sponge, knead, and let the
dough rise at least once, preferably twice.

**STEP III.**

**Cornmeal**

Cut the dough and shape the loaf-sized pieces into two
round loaves. Place them on a baking sheet dusted with
cornmeal.

**STEP IV.**

**1 egg, at room temperature**
    *mixed with*
**2 tablespoons water**

Slit the top of the loaves with a razor or sharp knife and
glaze them.

**STEP V.**

Bake the loaves in the lower part of a 400°F oven for 10
minutes and then at 350°F for 35 minutes, or until they test
done. Transfer the loaves to a cooling rack to cool completely.

# Triticale Bread with Cheese

Makes two 1¾-pound loaves and one 1¼-pound round

*Chewy and cheesy, even more delicious a week old.*

**STEP I.**

1/3 cup honey
2-1/2 cups lukewarm water
1/2 cup evaporated milk, heated to lukewarm
1 tablespoon active dry yeast
3 cups unbleached white bread flour

Prepare the sponge. Allow it to rise from 45 minutes to 2 hours.

**STEP II.**

1 tablespoon salt
1/3 cup olive oil
1-1/2 cups grated Cheddar or Gruyère cheese
3-3/4 cups triticale flour
1/2 to 1 cup unbleached white bread flour

**STEP III.**

Cut the dough and shape the loaf-sized pieces. Because of the tenderness of the dough, handle it gently.

**STEP IV.**

1 egg, at room temperature
  *mixed with*
2 tablespoons water

Slit the top of the loaves with a razor or sharp knife and glaze them.

**STEP V.**

Bake the loaves in a 350°F oven for 45 minutes, or until they test done. This bread is somewhat fragile. If you rotate the loaves during baking, handle them carefully. When they have finished baking, transfer the loaves to a cooling rack. The bread is perhaps even more delicious after mellowing a week in the refrigerator. It makes especially good toast that you do not even need to butter.

Makes two 2⅛-pound
standard loaves

# Cracked Wheat Bread

*Your own home-ground wheat kernels add crunch to a
light all-purpose bread.*

Cook 1 cup of cracked wheat kernels (bulgur) for 20 minutes. Drain, and process them in a food processor until they
are finely ground. Set aside.

STEP I.
**1/4 cup honey**
**1 cup lukewarm water**
**1 tablespoon active dry yeast**
**1 cup yogurt**
**1-1/2 cups unbleached white bread flour**

Prepare the sponge. Allow it to rise from 45 minutes to 2
hours.

STEP II.
**2 teaspoons salt**
**1/4 cup walnut oil**
**The cooked cracked wheat kernels**
**1 cup corn flour**
**3-1/4 to 4-1/4 cups unbleached white bread flour**

Add these ingredients to the sponge, knead, and let the
dough rise three times. After it has risen a third time, punch
the dough down and refrigerate it for 24 hours.

STEP III.
Punch the dough down again, cut it, and shape the loaf-
sized pieces into two 2⅛-pound standard loaves.

STEP IV.
**1 egg, at room temperature**
  *mixed with*
**2 tablespoons water**

Slit the top of the loaves with a razor or sharp knife and
glaze them.

STEP V.
Bake the loaves in a 350°F oven for 45 to 50 minutes, or until
they test done. Cool the loaves thoroughly on cooling
racks.

Makes one 1¾-pound
loaf and one 1¼-pound
round

# Maple-Oat Bread

*Creamy within, crispy without, with a subtly detectable
maple taste.*

Soak ½ cup of oat groats overnight in hot water or for 3
hours in boiling water. Process the groats in a food processor
for 2 minutes. They will be sticky, like a purée. Set aside.

STEP I.

**1/4 cup real maple syrup**
**1-1/2 cups lukewarm water**
**1 tablespoon active dry yeast**
**1/2 cup gluten flour**
**3/4 cups unbleached white bread flour**

Prepare the sponge. Allow it to rise from 45 minutes to 2
hours.

STEP II.

**1 egg, at room temperature, lightly beaten**
**2 teaspoons salt**
**1/4 cup safflower oil**
**1 cup oat flour**
**The processed oat groats**
**1-3/4 to 2-3/4 cups unbleached white bread flour**

Add these ingredients to the sponge, knead, and let the
dough rise at least once, preferably twice.

STEP III.

Cut the dough and shape the loaf-sized pieces into one
1¾-pound standard loaf and one 1¼-pound round.

STEP IV.

**Milk**

Slit the top of the loaves with a razor or sharp knife and glaze
them before and occasionally during baking with milk.

STEP V.

Bake the loaves in a 350°F oven for 55 minutes, or until
they test done. Transfer the loaves to a cooling rack to cool
completely.

Adapted from Abby Mandel's recipe published in the magazine, THE
PLEASURES OF COOKING, with permission of the publisher, the Cuisinart®
Cooking Club.

Makes two 1¾-pound
standard loaves and
one ¾-pound round

# Wheat Berry-Oatmeal Bread

*Everyone seems to like this bread for its chewy texture
and sweet taste of crushed wheat berries.*

Soak 1 cup of wheat berries in ½ cup of water overnight or
in boiling water for 3 hours. Process them in a food processor until they are finely ground. Set aside.

**STEP I.**
**1/2 cup honey**
**1-1/2 cups buttermilk, heated to lukewarm**
**1 tablespoon active dry yeast**
**2 cups whole-wheat flour**
**1/2 cup unbleached white bread flour**

Prepare the sponge. Allow it to rise from 45 minutes to 2
hours.

**STEP II.**
**1 tablespoon salt**
**1/4 cup corn oil**
**1/2 cup rolled oats**
**1/2 cup wheat germ**
**The processed wheat berries**
**1 cup whole-wheat flour**
**1-1/2 to 2-1/2 cups unbleached white bread flour**

Add these ingredients to the sponge, knead, and let the
dough rise at least once, preferably twice.

**STEP III.**
Cut the dough and shape the loaf-sized pieces into two
1¾-pound standard loaves and one ¾-pound round.

**STEP IV.**
**1 egg, at room temperature**
   ***mixed with***
**2 tablespoons water**

Slit the top of the loaves with a razor or sharp knife and
glaze them.

**STEP V.**
Bake the loaves in a 350°F oven for 50 to 60 minutes, or
until they test done. Transfer the loaves to a cooling rack to
cool completely.

# Spiced Wheat Berry Bread

*Raisins, cinnamon, and cloves embellish a traditional
wheat berry bread.*

Soak ½ cup of wheat berries in ¼ cup hot water overnight
or in boiling water for 3 hours. Process them in a food processor until they are finely ground. Set aside.

**STEP I.**
**1/4 cup malt syrup extract**
**1 cup buttermilk, heated to lukewarm**
**1 tablespoon active dry yeast**
**1 teaspoon cinnamon**
**1/8 teaspoon ground cloves**
**1/4 cup whole-wheat flour**
**1/2 cup unbleached white bread flour**

Prepare the sponge. Allow it to rise from 45 minutes to 2
hours.

**STEP II.**
**1-1/2 teaspoons salt**
**1/4 cup corn oil**
**The processed wheat berries**
**3/4 cup raisins**
**1/2 cup whole-wheat flour**
**3/4 to 1-3/4 cups unbleached white bread flour**

Add these ingredients to the sponge, knead, and let the
dough rise at least once, preferably twice.

**STEP III.** Cut the dough and shape the loaf-sized pieces into two
1⅛-pound rounds.

**STEP IV.**
**1 egg, at room temperature**
 *mixed with*
**2 tablespoons water**

Slit the top of the loaves with a razor or sharp knife and
glaze them.

**STEP V.** Bake the loaves in a 350°F oven for 30 to 35 minutes, or
until they test done. Transfer the loaves to a cooling rack to
cool completely.

Adapted from Abby Mandel's recipe published in the magazine, THE
PLEASURES OF COOKING, with permission of the publisher, the Cuisinart®
Cooking Club.

Makes one 1½-pound
loaf and one ¾-pound
braid

# Orange-Rye Berry Bread

*Cardamom and orange add a tinge of spice to the
bread's pungent berries.*

Soak ½ cup rye berries in hot water overnight or in boiling
water for 3 hours. Process them in a food processor until
they are finely ground. Set aside.

**STEP I.**

**1/4 cup firmly packed light brown sugar
1 cup orange juice, heated to lukewarm
1/4 cup powdered milk
1/2 teaspoon ground cardamom
1 teaspoon active dry yeast
1/2 to 3/4 cup unbleached white bread flour**

Prepare the sponge. Allow it to rise from 45 minutes to 2
hours.

**STEP II.**

**2 teaspoons salt
1/4 cup olive oil
The processed rye berries
2-1/4 to 3-1/4 cups unbleached white bread flour
Grated rind of 1 orange**

Add these ingredients to the sponge, knead, and let the
dough rise at least once, preferably twice.

**STEP III.**

Cut the dough and shape the loaf-sized pieces into one
1½-pound loaf and one ¾-pound braid, a shape that is
especially nice with this bread.

**STEP IV.**

**Orange juice**

Slit the top of the loaves with a razor or sharp knife and
glaze them before, once or twice during, and again after
baking with orange juice.

**STEP V.**

Bake the loaves in a 350°F oven for 40 to 45 minutes, or
until they test done. Cool them thoroughly on cooling
racks.

Adapted from Abby Mandel's recipe published in the magazine, THE
PLEASURES OF COOKING, with permission of the publisher, the Cuisinart®
Cooking Club.

# Onion Bread with Triticale Berries

*Triticale is a hybrid of rye and wheat. Its berries, along with onions and caraway, make a smooth, savory dough that you might like to shape into buns for sandwiches.*

Soak ½ cup of triticale berries overnight in hot water or in boiling water for 3 hours. Process them in a food processor until they are finely ground. Set aside.

**STEP I.**    1/4 cup honey
1 cup buttermilk, heated to lukewarm
1 tablespoon active dry yeast
3/4 cup unbleached white bread flour

Prepare the sponge. Allow it to rise from 45 minutes to 2 hours.

**STEP II.**    1-1/2 teaspoons salt
1/4 cup unsalted butter, softened
2 medium onions chopped fine and sautéed in
    butter until they are soft but not brown; this
    will take about 5 minutes
The processed triticale berries
2-1/4 to 3-1/4 cups unbleached white bread flour
1/2 tablespoon caraway seed

Add these ingredients to the sponge, knead, and let the dough rise at least once, preferably twice. The dough will be very moist. If necessary add a bit more white flour.

**STEP III.**    Cut the dough and shape the loaf-sized pieces into two 1½-pound rounds or standard 4½-by-8½-inch loaves.

**STEP IV.**    1 egg, at room temperature
    *mixed with*
2 tablespoons water

Slit the top of the loaves with a razor or sharp knife and glaze them.

**STEP V.**    Bake the loaves in a 350°F oven for 40 to 50 minutes, or until they test done. Transfer the loaves to a cooling rack to cool completely.

Adapted from Abby Mandel's recipe published in the magazine, THE PLEASURES OF COOKING, with permission of the publisher, the Cuisinart® Cooking Club.

Makes two 1½-pound
loaves and assorted rolls

# Buckwheat Bread

*Buckwheat, a plant with heart-shaped leaves, is culti-vated for the satisfying nourishment in its three-sided seeds. Anything made with buckwheat, including this bread, is marked by its exotic character.*

Pan roast ½ cup of buckwheat flour in a dry skillet, stirring constantly, until it darkens in color by several shades. Set aside.

Heat ⅔ cup buckwheat groats in a dry skillet with 1 egg. Cook while stirring until the grains are coated with egg and no longer stick together. Add 2 cups of hot water, cover, and bring the groats to a boil. Simmer them for 20 minutes or until the groats are fluffy and tender. Set aside.

*STEP I.*

**1/4 cup firmly packed light brown sugar**
**1/2 cup lukewarm water**
**1-1/2 cups milk scalded and cooled to lukewarm**
**1 tablespoon active dry yeast**
**2 cups unbleached white bread flour**

Prepare the sponge. Allow it to rise from 45 minutes to 2 hours.

*STEP II.*

**2 teaspoons salt**
**1/4 unsalted butter, softened**
**The roasted buckwheat flour**
**The cooked buckwheat groats**
**1 to 2 cups unbleached white bread flour**

Add these ingredients to the sponge, knead, and let the dough rise at least once, preferably twice.

*STEP III.*

Cut the dough and shape the loaf-sized pieces into two standard 4½-by-8½-inch loaves and assorted rolls.

*STEP IV.*

**1 egg, at room temperature**
  *mixed with*
**2 tablespoons water**

Slit the top of the loaves with a razor or sharp knife and glaze them.

**STEP V.**    Bake the loaves in a 375°F oven for 40 minutes, then at 350°F for 10 minutes; the rolls at 375°F for about 25 minutes, at which point check them for doneness. Transfer the loaves and rolls to a cooling rack to cool completely.

---

Makes two 1-pound,
10-ounce loaves

# Buttermilk Oat Bread

*A tangy, chewy, long-lasting loaf*

Soak 2⅓ cups of rolled oats overnight at room temperature in 1¼ cups buttermilk. Set aside.

**STEP I.**    **1/3 cup unsulphured molasses**
**1-1/4 cups buttermilk, heated to lukewarm**
**1 tablespoon active dry yeast**
**1/2 cup gluten flour**
**1 cup unbleached white bread flour**

Prepare the sponge. Allow it to rise from 45 minutes to 2 hours.

**STEP II.**    **2 teaspoons salt**
**3 tablespoons unsalted butter, softened**
**The soaked rolled oats, with the buttermilk**
**1 cup oat flour**
**3/4 to 1-3/4 cups unbleached white bread flour**

Add these ingredients to the sponge, knead, and let the dough rise at least once, preferably twice.

**STEP III.**    Cut the dough and shape the loaf-sized pieces into two standard 4½-by-8½-inch loaves.

**STEP IV.**    **1 egg, at room temperature**
*mixed with*
**2 tablespoons water**

Slit the top of the loaves with a razor or sharp knife and glaze them.

**STEP V.**    Bake the loaves in a 350°F oven for 50 to 60 minutes, or until they test done. Transfer the loaves to a cooling rack to cool completely.

# Barley Bread with Seeds

*Sunflower seeds and nuggets of carrots enrich a moist
and earthy bread. It lends itself to sandwiches (especially
ones with alfalfa sprouts) and hearty winter soups.*

Roast ½ cup of sunflower seeds for 10 minutes in a 400°F
oven. Set aside. Pan roast 1½ cups of barley flour in 1 tablespoon of sesame oil, stirring constantly, until the flour is
darkened. Set aside.

*STEP I.*     **1/4 cup malt syrup extract**
**2 cups lukewarm water**
**1 tablespoon active dry yeast**
**1/2 cup powdered milk**
**1 cup whole-wheat flour**
**1-1/2 cups unbleached white bread flour**

Prepare the sponge. Allow it to rise from 45 minutes to 2
hours.

*STEP II.*     **2 teaspoons salt**
**1/4 cup sunflower or sesame oil**
**The roasted barley flour**
**1 cup mashed, cooked carrots (about 2 large
  carrots) with a few small chunks left in for
  taste and appearance**
**The roasted sunflower seeds**
**1/2 cup whole-wheat flour**
**1-1/4 to 2-1/4 cups unbleached white bread flour**

Add these ingredients to the sponge, knead, and let the
dough rise at least once, preferably twice.

*STEP III.*     Cut the dough and shape the loaf-sized pieces into two
2-pound rounds.

*STEP IV.*     **1 egg, at room temperature**
  *mixed with*
**2 tablespoons water**

Slit the top of the loaves with a razor or sharp knife and
glaze them.

*STEP V.*     Bake the loaves in a 350°F oven for 45 minutes, or until the
loaves test done. Cool them thoroughly on cooling racks.

# Cornmeal-Millet Bread

*A pleasantly crunchy, mild yet sweet loaf.*

STEP I.
1/2 cup honey
1/2 cup lukewarm water
2 cups buttermilk, heated to lukewarm
1 tablespoon active dry yeast
3 cups unbleached white bread flour

Prepare the sponge. Allow it to rise from 45 minutes to 2 hours.

STEP II.
1 tablespoon salt
1/3 cup corn oil
2 cups yellow cornmeal
1 cup whole millet—If you would like slightly less crunchiness, soak the millet in water for half an hour before adding it to the sponge
2-1/4 to 3-1/4 cups unbleached white bread flour

Add these ingredients to the sponge, knead, and let the dough rise at least once, preferably twice.

STEP III.
Cut the dough and shape the loaf-sized pieces into three standard 4½-by-8½-inch loaves.

STEP IV.
1 egg, at room temperature
*mixed with*
1 teaspoon water

Slit the top of the loaves with a razor or sharp knife and glaze them.

STEP V.
Bake the loaves in a 350°F oven for 35 to 40 minutes, or until they test done. Transfer the loaves to a cooling rack to cool completely.

Makes two standard
4½-by-8½-inch loaves
or one round bun bread

# Rippled Bread

*Buns of dark and light dough from an array of whole-some ingredients yield curiously marbled slices that are diverting in appearance.*

**STEP I.**  *Dark Dough*

**1/4 cup honey**
**1-1/2 cups lukewarm water**
**1 tablespoon active dry yeast**
**1/2 cup gluten flour**
**1 cup unbleached white bread flour**

*Light Dough*

**1/4 cup honey**
**1 cup lukewarm water**
**1 tablespoon active dry yeast**
**1 cup unbleached white bread flour**

Prepare the sponges. Allow them to rise from 45 minutes to 2 hours.

**STEP II.**  *Dark Dough*

**2 teaspoons salt**
**1/4 cup walnut oil**
**1 cup chopped walnuts**
**1/2 cup buckwheat flour**
**1/2 cup corn flour**
**1/2 cup rye flour**
**1/4 cup whole-wheat flour, or as much as necessary
for kneading**

*Light Dough*

**1 teaspoon salt**
**1/4 cup walnut oil**
**2 cups unbleached white bread flour, or as much
as necessary for kneading**

Add these ingredients to the sponges, knead, and let the doughs rise at least once, preferably twice. The dark dough, as a result of the gluten flour, will be thick and have a lot of spunk at the beginning of Step II.

**STEP III.**    Cut the dough and shape the loaf-sized pieces in one of the following ways:

> Form each dough separately into 6 balls and place 3 dark and 3 light balls side by side in a loaf pan; a total of 6 balls per loaf.

> Form 16 rolls. In a round, well-buttered cake pan, place the rolls so that one is in the center, 5 surround it, and 10 surround the 5. Alternate the dark and light rolls according to your taste. Do not allow the 10 outer rolls to touch the edges of the cake pan.

**STEP IV.**    **1 egg white, at room temperature**
*mixed with*
**1 teaspoon water**
**Finely chopped walnuts for topping**

Do not slit the loaves. Glaze them and sprinkle the tops with finely chopped walnuts.

**STEP V.**    Bake the loaves in a 425°F oven for 15 minutes and then at 375°F for 20 to 25 minutes, or until the tops are golden and the loaves test done. Transfer the loaves to a cooling rack to cool completely.

Makes one bundt pan
of bread

## Monkey Bread

*Little balls of dough rolled in a butter-currant sauce frost themselves during baking. Serve it warm and pull apart in clumps. Variations follow the recipe.*

**STEP I.**

**1 cup sugar**
**1-1/2 cups milk, scalded and cooled to lukewarm**
**1 tablespoon active dry yeast**
**3 cups unbleached white bread flour**

Prepare the sponge. Allow it to rise from 45 minutes to 2 hours.

**3/4 cup currants with rum or orange juice to cover.**

Let the currants soak while proceeding to Step II.

**STEP II.**

**1 teaspoon salt**
**1/4 cup unsalted butter, softened**
**3 eggs + 2 yolks, at room temperature, lightly beaten**
**5 to 6 cups unbleached white bread flour**

Add these ingredients to the sponge, knead, and let the dough rise at least once, preferably twice.

**STEP III.**

*Butter-currant filling*
**1/4 cup unsalted butter**
**3/4 cup firmly packed brown sugar**
**The currants, drained**

Melt the butter, brown sugar, and currants together in a saucepan and set the mixture aside. Butter a bundt pan. Pinch off portions of dough the size of golf balls. Place ⅓ of the melted filling mixture in the bottom of the buttered bundt pan. Top this with ½ of the balls and pour ½ of the remaining filling mixture over the balls. Cover the filling with the remaining balls and pour the remaining filling over them. Cover the pan and let the dough rise until it reaches the top.

**STEP V.**

Bake the bread at 325°F for 45 to 60 minutes, covering the top with a foil tent if it seems to be browning too quickly. Be sure the bread tests done before removing it from the oven. Use a cake testing pin or metal skewer, which, when inserted into the center of the bread, should come out clean and free of particles. Remember what the finished bread looks like so that in the future, you will be able to test for doneness by sight. Transfer the bread to a cooling rack to cool briefly before serving warm.

**VARIATIONS**

*Lemon filling*
**1/4 cup unsalted butter**
**1/2 cup sugar**
**1 teaspoon freshly grated nutmeg**
**Grated rind of 2 lemons**

Melt the butter, sugar, nutmeg, and grated lemon rind together in a saucepan. Use as directed in the main recipe.

*Garlic-sesame filling*
**1/3 cup unsalted butter**
**1 clove garlic, crushed**
**3 tablespoons sesame seed**

Melt the butter and garlic in a small saucepan over low heat. Let the mixture cook 2 minutes more, being careful that the butter does not burn. Stir in the sesame seed and use as directed in the main recipe.

Makes one 8-inch cake

# Deckered Cream Cake

*This cake, served piping hot, is sliced into layers that are spread with butter or scalded cream, broiled briefly, and sandwiched back together.*

**STEP I.**
**2 tablespoons sugar**
**1/3 cup + 1 tablespoon lukewarm water**
**1 tablespoon active dry yeast**
**3/4 cup unbleached white bread flour**

Prepare the sponge. Allow it to rise from 45 minutes to 2 hours.

**STEP II.**
**1/2 teaspoon salt**
**1/2 cup + 2 tablespoons unsalted butter, softened**
**4 egg yolks, at room temperature**
**1/3 + 1 tablespoon heavy cream**
**2-1/2 to 3-1/2 cups unbleached white bread flour**

Add these ingredients to the sponge, knead, and let the dough rise at least once, preferably twice.

**STEP III.**
Place the dough in a buttered 8-inch brioche or charlotte mold and let it rise until it reaches the top of the mold.

**STEP IV.**
**1 egg**
  *mixed with*
**1 teaspoon water**

Brush the glaze on top of the cake.

**STEP V.**
**1/2 cup unsalted butter, softened**
  *or*
**1/2 cup cream, scalded**

Bake the cake at 350°F for 45 to 55 minutes. As soon as the cake tests done, remove it from the mold. Slice it in half horizontally and spread each half with softened butter or scalded cream. Place the halves briefly under a broiler, buttered or creamed sides up, then piece them together again. Serve the cake piping hot.

# Butter Crunch Coffeecake

*Almonds and walnuts enrich a scrumptious version of this old-fashioned, crumb-topped favorite.*

STEP I.

**1/2 cup sugar**
**3/4 cup milk, scalded and cooled to lukewarm**
**1 tablespoon active dry yeast**
**Grated rind of 1 lemon**
**1 teaspoon vanilla**
**1-1/2 cups unbleached white bread flour**

Prepare the sponge. Allow it to rise from 45 minutes to 2 hours.

STEP II.

**3 large eggs at room temperature, lightly beaten**
**1/2 cup unsalted butter, softened**
**1 teaspoon salt**
**2-1/2 to 3-1/2 cups unbleached white bread flour**

Add these ingredients to the sponge, knead, and let the dough rise at least once, preferably twice.

STEP III.

*Topping*
**1/3 cup butter, unsalted, at room temperature**
**1/2 cup sugar**
**3/4 cups firmly packed dark brown sugar**
**Pinch salt**
**1/3 cup ground almonds**
**1/3 cup ground walnuts**
**1/2 teaspoon cinnamon**
**1/2 teaspoon vanilla**

In a small bowl cream the butter, sugar, and brown sugar. Add the salt, almonds, walnuts, cinnamon, and vanilla and set the mixture aside. Spread the dough into a 12-by-9-by-2-inch buttered baking dish. When it has risen to the top, drop the topping by teaspoons onto the dough.

STEP V.

With a cookie sheet under the baking dish to catch spills, bake the cake at 375°F for 35 minutes, or until its top is golden brown. Transfer the cake to a cooling rack.

# Coffeewreath with Pistachios

*A charming wreath filled and topped with lovely green pistachios.*

**STEP I.**
**1/2 cup sugar**
**1 cup milk, scalded and cooled to lukewarm**
**1 tablespoon active dry yeast**
**1-1/2 cups unbleached white bread flour**

Prepare the sponge. Allow it to rise from 45 minutes to 2 hours.

**STEP II.**
**1 teaspoon salt**
**1/4 cup unsalted butter, softened**
**2 to 3 cups unbleached white bread flour**

Add these ingredients to the sponge, knead, and let the dough rise at least once, preferably twice.

**STEP III.**
*Filling*
**2 tablespoons melted butter**
**1/3 cup sugar**
**1 cup skinned, coarsely chopped pistachio nuts**

(Skin the nuts by heating on a cookie sheet in a 275°F oven for about 4 minutes; place the warm nuts on a flat surface and rub, discarding the skins).

On a floured surface roll the dough into a 12-by-18-inch rectangle. Drizzle it to within 1 inch of the edge with 2 tablespoons of melted butter. Sprinkle it with sugar and spread the nuts evenly over the surface. Beginning from the wide end, roll it as you would a jelly roll. Pinch the ends together. Place the wreath on a buttered baking sheet.

**STEP IV.**
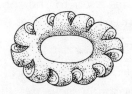
**1 egg, at room temperature**
*mixed with*
**1 tablespoon milk**

Cut the wreath at 1-inch intervals ¾ of the way through. Twist the slices slightly and let them rise until they have doubled in size. Brush the entire top with glaze.

**STEP V.**
Bake the wreath at 350°F for 30 to 35 minutes. Transfer the wreath to a rack to cool slightly before serving warm.

Makes 1 loaf

# Chocolate Swirled Bread

*Another marbled bread, this swirly one is for chocolate lovers.*

**STEP I.**    **1/2 cup sugar**
**2 cups milk, scalded and cooled to lukewarm**
**1 tablespoon active dry yeast**
**2-1/2 cups unbleached white bread flour**

Prepare the sponge. Allow it to rise from 45 minutes to 2 hours.

**STEP II.**    **1 teaspoon salt**
**1/2 cup unsalted butter, softened**
**3 egg yolks, at room temperature**
**2-1/2 to 3-1/2 cups unbleached white bread flour**

Add these ingredients to the sponge, knead, and let the dough rise at least once, preferably twice.

**STEP III.**    *Filling*
**6 ounces grated semisweet chocolate**
**1/4 cup unsalted butter, melted**
**1/2 cup sugar**

Divide the dough into two portions. Knead the grated chocolate into one. On a floured surface, roll the plain half of the dough into a 8-by-15-inch rectangle. Brush it with melted butter and sprinkle it evenly with sugar. Roll the chocolate half of the dough into a rectangle of the same size. Place the chocolate half on top of the sugared half and, starting at the wide end, roll both together tightly as you would a jelly roll. Pinch the ends together. Place the bread in a buttered 4-quart mold, cover it, and let it rise until it reaches the top of the mold.

**STEP IV.**    Bake the bread at 325°F for 45 to 55 minutes, or until it tests done. Transfer the bread to a cooling rack.

# Braid of Fruit

*A bread with the surprise of a delicious stuffing in each strand of the braid. Choose from four different fruit or nut fillings or invent your own.*

**STEP I.**
1 tablespoon sugar
1/4 cup lukewarm water
3/4 cup milk, scalded and cooled to lukewarm
1 tablespoon active dry yeast
1-1/2 cups unbleached white bread flour

Prepare the sponge. Allow it to rise from 45 minutes to 2 hours.

**STEP II.**
1 teaspoon salt
3/4 cup unsalted butter, softened
3 eggs, at room temperature
4-1/2 to 5-1/2 cups unbleached white bread flour

Add these ingredients to the sponge, knead, and let the dough rise at least once, preferably twice.

**STEP III.**
*Filling*

Instructions for four fillings follow the recipe.

Dust your work surface lightly with flour and roll out the dough into a 26-by-10-by-¼-inch rectangle. Let the dough relax for 5 minutes. Place about 3 tablespoons of filling across the width of the dough leaving a 1-inch margin at the bottom and a ½-inch margin on either side. Lift the bottom edge over the filling and roll the dough *snugly* until there is a 1-inch overlap. Cut off the rolled piece, pinch the seam and ends tightly, roll it gently back and forth to form a strand and leave it resting, seam-side down, while you shape the other two strands. Lay the 3 strands parallel to one another and braid them, beginning from the center and working out to each end. Moisten the dough at the ends and pinch them together. Cover the braid and let it rise for half an hour.

**STEP IV.**
1 egg, at room temperature
  *mixed with*
1 tablespoon milk
Poppyseed *(optional)*

Brush the braid with glaze and sprinkle it with poppyseed if desired.

**STEP V.**   Bake the braid in a 400°F oven for 25 minutes, checki
during the final 10 minutes for overbrowning. Cover the
braid with foil if it is browning too rapidly. Transfer the
braid to a rack to cool slightly before serving warm.

**VARIATIONS**

*Almond paste*

**12 ounces almond paste**
**3 tablespoons unsalted butter, softened**
**6 tablespoons powdered sugar**
**3 egg whites, at room temperature**

Combine the almond paste, butter, powdered sugar, and egg
whites in a food processor or blender and process or blend
them until they are smooth. Use ⅓ of the recipe for each
strand of the braid.

*Prune filling*

**3-1/2 cups chopped, dried prunes**
**1/2 cup honey**
**3/4 cup orange juice**
**1/2 teaspoon cloves**
**1 teaspoon cinnamon**

Combine the prunes, honey, orange juice, cloves, and cinnamon in a large, heavy-bottomed saucepan. Cook them
over low heat until the prunes begin to fall apart and the
mixture masses. Use ⅓ of the recipe for each strand of the
braid.

*Poppyseed filling*

**3 cups ground poppyseed**
**3/4 cup milk**
**1/3 cup honey**
**2 tablespoons sugar**
**3 tablespoons unsalted butter**
**1 teaspoon cinnamon**

Combine the poppyseed, milk, honey, and sugar in a large,
heavy-bottomed saucepan and cook them over low heat for
5 minutes. Stir in the butter and cinnamon. Use ⅓ of the
recipe for each strand of the braid.

*Walnut filling*

**1 cup sour cream**
**1/2 cup + 1 tablespoon honey, heated**
**1 teaspoon vanilla**

**3 cups walnuts, chopped very fine**
**3 egg whites, at room temperature**
**Pinch of cream of tartar**
**Pinch of salt**

In a large bowl, combine the sour cream, honey, vanilla, and walnuts. In a separate, smaller bowl beat the egg whites with the cream of tartar and salt until they hold stiff peaks. Gently fold the egg whites into the walnut mixture. Divide the recipe in 3 and use ⅓ for each strand of the braid.

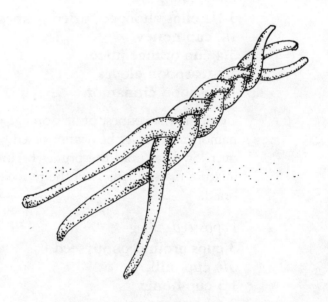

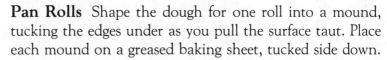

# ROLLS AND BUNS

Any bread dough can be made into rolls. A standard-size loaf's worth (1¾ pounds) will make fourteen 2-ounce rolls. The dough should be prepared in the same way as bread but, instead of forming a loaf, shape the dough into a log about 1½ to 2 inches in diameter. Slice the log into portions of the size roll desired and shape the portions attractively. Here are instructions on how to prepare a few of the more classic styles.

**Pan Rolls** Shape the dough for one roll into a mound, tucking the edges under as you pull the surface taut. Place each mound on a greased baking sheet, tucked side down.

**Clover Leaf Rolls** Divide the dough for one roll into three pieces. Shape each piece into a ball and place all three balls into one greased muffin cup.

**Crescent Rolls** Instead of rolling the dough into a log, use a rolling pin and roll it into a circle about ¼ of an inch thick. Brush the top with melted butter and cut it into triangular wedges. Starting from the outer edge, roll up each triangle, tucking the small inner end under. Curve the roll into a half-moon, or crescent, and place it on a greased baking sheet.

**Coiled Rolls** Roll each portion of the dough into a rope ½ an inch in diameter and approximately 6 inches long. Taking one rope, or two held together as if they were one, knot it and place the knot on a greased baking sheet. Each knot makes one roll.

**Twists** Alternately, take two ropes, each 4 inches long, and twist them, pinching the ends together. Place the twists 1 inch apart on a greased baking sheet. Each twist makes one roll.

**Parker House Rolls** Shape the dough for one roll into a ball about 2½ inches in diameter. Flatten the ball and make a crease down the center with a floured spatula. Butter one half of the surface (the part on one side of the crease) and fold the other half over it, pressing the edges carefully together. The edges do not have to meet exactly. Place the irregular half circles 1 inch apart on a greased baking sheet and brush them again with butter.

**Split Rolls**  Shape a portion of dough into the size of a golf ball, sprinkle it lightly with flour and split it almost in two with a blow from the side of your palm. There will be two ridges with a crevice down the center. Turn the rolls upside down to rise, then right side up to bake.

**Button Rolls**  Shape the dough for one roll into a cylindrical oblong 4 to 5 inches long and 2 to 3 inches wide. Use your palms to make a completely smooth surface. Then, holding a pair of wet scissors at a 45° angle, make 4 to 5 triangular cuts about 1 inch long down the center of the roll. The points of the triangle will rise during baking and form buttons.

# Alternate Slitting Patterns for Rolls

A single razor stroke across the top of the roll.

Tops snipped with a pair of wet scissors at angles pointing in opposite directions to give a saw-tooth effect.

Tops snipped twice with a pair of wet scissors to form a cross.

After the rolls have been shaped, let them rise for 20 minutes. Glaze them, sprinkle the tops with seed and bake them for about 25 minutes at 375°F, or until the rolls are golden brown. Because they are small, rolls have a larger proportion of crust. Undoubtedly you will want to develop this. Choose your glaze carefully in order to produce the desired texture (see the Glazing Chart on p. 61). Remember that the manner in which the unbaked rolls are placed on the baking sheet will also determine the texture of the crust. If the rolls are close together, the crusts will be softer than if they were further apart. See p. 63 for other means of varying the crusts.

Make a large batch of dough. Refrigerate it and, each night, pull off a portion for dinner rolls, varying the embellishments according to your menu.

Or, make your own "ready-to-serve" rolls. Prepare the rolls for baking as usual. Then bake them at 275°F until the dough is firm but uncolored. Remove the partially baked rolls from the oven, cool them thoroughly, wrap them well, and store them in the refrigerator or freezer. When you are ready to use the rolls, brush them lightly with the glaze of your choice (no need to defrost) and bake them in a 400°F oven until they are nicely browned.

Makes 24 rolls

## Swiss Breakfast Rolls

These crusty rolls must be those that Heinrich Böll's heroine, Leni Pfeiffer, so diligently sought out for herself:

> A few additional details must be supplied concerning Leni's daily habits. She enjoys eating, but in moderation; her main meal is breakfast, for which she positively must have two crisp fresh rolls, a fresh, soft-boiled egg, a little butter, one or two tablespoons of jam (more precisely: the plum purée known elsewhere as *Powidl*), strong coffee that she mixes with hot milk, very little sugar; midday dinner scarcely interests her: soup and a modest dessert are all she wants; then in the evening she has a cold meal, some bread, two or three slices, salad, sausage and cold meat when she can afford them. What Leni cares about most is the fresh

rolls; rather than have them delivered she picks them out for herself, not by fingering them, merely by inspecting their color; there is nothing—in the way of food, at least—that she hates as much as limp rolls.[6]

**STEP I.**

**2 tablespoons sugar**
**2 cups milk, scalded and cooled to lukewarm**
**1 tablespoon active dry yeast**
**2-1/2 cups unbleached white bread flour**

Prepare the sponge. Allow it to rise from 45 minutes to 2 hours.

**STEP II.**

**1 teaspoon salt**
**1/4 cup unsalted butter or lard, softened**
**2-1/2 to 3-1/2 cups unbleached white bread flour**

Add these ingredients to the sponge, knead, and let the dough rise at least once, preferably twice.

**STEP III.**

Divide the dough into 24 pieces. Form each piece into a ball and roll each ball with your hands into a smooth 4-inch cylinder.

**STEP IV.**

**1 egg, at room temperature**
 *mixed with*
**Pinch of salt**

Place the cylinders about 3 inches apart on a buttered baking sheet. Glaze them with half the glaze and let them rise until they have almost doubled in size. Brush them again with the remaining glaze. Then, with a pair of wet scissors at a 45° angle, make 5 small snips across the top of each roll.

**STEP V.**

Bake the rolls at 375°F for 30 to 40 minutes, or until they have browned nicely. Transfer them to cooling racks.

# Cornmeal Oatmeal Rolls

*A homey, highly textured dinner roll.*

**STEP I.**
**1/4 cup honey**
**1-1/4 cups milk, scalded and cooled to lukewarm**
**1 tablespoon active dry yeast**
**1/4 cup brewers' yeast**
**2 cups unbleached white bread flour**

Prepare the sponge. Allow it to rise from 45 minutes to 2 hours.

**STEP II.**
**1 teaspoon salt**
**1/4 cup corn oil**
**1 egg, at room temperature, lightly beaten**
**1 cup yellow cornmeal**
**1/2 cup rolled oats**
**2 to 2-1/2 cups unbleached white bread flour**

Add these ingredients to the sponge, knead, and let the dough rise at least once, preferably twice.

**STEP III.** Cut the dough into roll-sized pieces.

**STEP IV.**
**1 egg, at room temperature**
*mixed with*
**1 teaspoon water**

Slit the rolls and brush them with glaze.

**STEP V.** Bake the rolls in a 375°F oven for about 20 minutes or until they are golden. Transfer them to cooling racks.

# Parsley Scallion Rolls

*Fresh herbs and scallions spiral inside and on top of these exquisite rolls for brunch or buffet.*

**STEP I.**

**2 tablespoons sugar**
**1 cup milk, scalded and cooled to lukewarm**
**1 tablespoon active dry yeast**
**1-1/2 cups unbleached white bread flour**

Prepare the sponge. Allow it to rise from 45 minutes to 2 hours.

**STEP II.**

**1 teaspoon salt**
**1/2 cup vegetable shortening, softened**
**1 egg, at room temperature**
**2 to 3 cups unbleached white bread flour**

Add these ingredients to the sponge, knead, and let the dough rise at least once, preferably twice.

**STEP III.**

*Filling*
**1/2 cup unsalted butter, softened**
**2/3 cup minced fresh parsley**
**1/2 cup minced scallions**

Divide the dough into 2 portions. Roll each half into an 8-by-12-inch rectangle and spread it with 2 tablespoons of butter. Meanwhile, combine the parsley and scallions in a bowl. Divide the mixture into 3 parts and sprinkle each rectangle with one portion. Combine the remaining portion with the remaining ¼ cup butter. Mix this well and set it aside. Roll each rectangle as you would a jelly roll and cut it into 12 pieces. Place the pieces in well-buttered muffin cups and let them rise until they reach the top of the cups.

**STEP V.**

Bake the rolls at 350°F for 20 to 25 minutes, or until they have browned well. As you remove them from the oven, spread the top of each roll with the reserved parsley, scallion, and butter mixture.

Makes 30 rolls

# Coconut Cream Rolls

*Coconut, pineapple, and macadamia nuts lend this otherwise traditional dinner roll a special Hawaiian character.*

STEP I.
1 tablespoon sugar
3/4 cup coconut-pineapple juice, heated to lukewarm
3 tablespoons cream of coconut (heat the contents of an 8-ounce can to lukewarm)
1 tablespoon active dry yeast
1-1/2 cups unbleached white bread flour

Prepare the sponge. Allow it to rise from 45 minutes to 2 hours.

STEP II.
1 teaspoon salt
1/4 cup unsalted butter, softened
2 eggs, at room temperature
The remainder of the 8-ounce can of coconut cream
1 cup coarsely ground macadamia nuts
4-1/2 cups unbleached white bread flour

Add these ingredients to the sponge, knead, and let the dough rise at least once, preferably twice.

STEP III.
Divide the dough into 30 balls. Press each ball firmly into a bun or muffin cup, preferably one with designs on the sides. Cover them and let them rise until they reach the top of the cups.

STEP IV.
1 egg, at room temperature
*mixed with*
1 tablespoon milk

Brush the rolls with glaze.

STEP V.
Bake the rolls at 375°F for 25 minutes or until they are lightly browned. Transfer them to cooling racks.

Makes about 24 rolls

# Butterscotch Pecan Rolls

*Sticky and delicious, these upside-down rolls are filled and garnished with pecans.*

**STEP I.**
1/2 cup sugar
1 cup milk, scalded and cooled to lukewarm
1 tablespoon active dry yeast
1-1/2 cups unbleached white bread flour

Prepare the sponge. Allow to rise 45 minutes to 2 hours.

**STEP II.**
1 teaspoon salt
1/2 cup unsalted butter, softened
2 eggs, at room temperature, lightly beaten
3-1/2 to 4 cups unbleached white bread flour

Add these ingredients to the sponge, knead, and let the dough rise at least once, preferably twice.

**STEP III.** *Filling*
1/4 cup melted unsalted butter
1/2 cup firmly packed brown sugar
1/2 cup ground pecans

*Butterscotch mixture*
1/3 cup unsalted butter, melted
2/3 cup firmly packed brown sugar
Pecan halves

Divide the dough into 2 pieces. Roll each piece into a 8-by-12-inch rectangle. Spread half of the filling mixture on each rectangle to within 1 inch of the edges. Beginning with the long end, roll the rectangle jelly-roll fashion, leaving the seam side down. Cut each roll into 1-inch slices. For the butterscotch mixture, combine the melted butter, brown sugar, and pecan halves. Place a heaping teaspoon of the mixture on the bottom of 24 well-buttered muffin cups. Do not use paper liners. Place 1 roll slice in each muffin cup. Cover the rolls and let them rise until they reach the top of the cups.

**STEP V.**
Bake the rolls at 375°F for 20 to 25 minutes, or until they are golden. Remove them from the oven and allow them to stand for 1 minute. Then invert them quickly onto cooling racks.

# Sweet Potato Ginger Crescents

*Glazed or plain, spicy russet crescents are ideal for winter festivities.*

**STEP I.**
1/4 cup sugar
1-1/2 cups milk, scalded and cooled to lukewarm
1 tablespoon active dry yeast
2 teaspoons freshly grated ginger
2 teaspoons freshly grated orange rind
1/4 teaspoon freshly grated nutmeg
2-1/4 cups unbleached white bread flour

Prepare the sponge. Allow to rise 45 minutes to 2 hours.

**STEP II.**
2 teaspoons salt
3/4 cup unsalted butter, softened
1-1/2 cups unpeeled sweet potatoes, cooked and mashed
5-1/2 to 6-1/2 cups unbleached white bread flour

Add these ingredients to the sponge, knead, and let the dough rise at least once, preferably twice.

**STEP III.** Shape the dough into crescents (for shaping instructions, see p. 131). Place the crescents about 2 inches apart on a buttered baking sheet. Cover them and let them rise until they have doubled in size.

**STEP IV.**
1 egg, at room temperature
 *mixed with*
1 teaspoon water

Brush the crescents with glaze.

**STEP V.** Bake the crescents at 375°F for 15 to 20 minutes, or until they are nicely browned. Transfer them to cooling racks.

**VARIATION**
1-1/2 cups sifted powdered sugar
1 teaspoon grated orange rind
1/4 teaspoon freshly grated nutmeg
2 to 4 tablespoons heavy cream

To serve these rolls for breakfast or brunch, eliminate step IV. Mix all of the above ingredients except the cream together in a small bowl. Add cream to make the desired consistency. Drizzle the glaze over the baked crescents.

Makes about 30 buns

# Currant Buns

*An orangy, spicy egg dough encases currants steeped and plumped.*

Soak ½ cup currants in enough rum or orange juice to cover them.

STEP I.
**2 tablespoons sugar**
**2/3 cup milk, scalded and cooled to lukewarm**
**1 tablespoon active dry yeast**
**1 cup unbleached white bread flour**

Prepare the sponge. Allow it to rise from 45 minutes to 2 hours.

STEP II.
**1 teaspoon salt**
**1 cup unsalted butter, softened**
**2 teaspoons grated orange rind**
**1 teaspoon allspice**
**3 to 4 cups unbleached white bread flour**

Add these ingredients to the sponge, knead, and let the dough rise at least once, preferably twice.

STEP III.
*Filling*
**3 tablespoons unsalted melted butter**
**1/3 cup + 1 tablespoon firmly packed brown sugar**
**The currants, drained and patted dry**

Divide the dough in half and roll each half into a 10-by-15-inch rectangle. In a small bowl, combine the melted butter, brown sugar, and currants. On one rectangle spread half of the filling to within 1 inch of the edges, fold the dough into thirds, then turn it one quarter turn. Reroll it into a 10-by-15-inch rectangle. Beginning from the long edge, roll the rectangle as you would a jelly roll. Cut it into 1-inch slices. Repeat the procedure with the remaining half of the dough and place each slice in a well-buttered muffin cup. Do not use paper liners. Let the buns rise until the dough reaches the top of the cups.

STEP V.
Bake the buns at 375°F for 15 to 20 minutes or until they are golden brown. Transfer the buns to a cooling rack.

# Hot Cross Buns

*These buns are light and slightly sweet, perfect spread with lemon curd (the recipe for which follows).*

**STEP I.**
3 tablespoons firmly packed light brown sugar
1-1/4 cups milk, scalded and cooled to lukewarm
1 tablespoon active dry yeast
1 teaspoon cinnamon
3/4 teaspoon freshly grated nutmeg
1/4 teaspoon allspice
1/4 teaspoon cloves
2 cups unbleached white bread flour

Prepare the sponge. Allow it to rise from 45 minutes to 2 hours.

**STEP II.**
1/2 teaspoon salt
3 tablespoons unsalted butter, softened
2 eggs, at room temperature, lightly beaten
1/2 cup currants
3-1/2 to 4-1/2 cups unbleached white bread flour

Add these ingredients to the sponge, knead, and let the dough rise at least once, preferably twice.

**STEP III.**
Divide the dough into 24 pieces. Round each piece into a bun. Arrange the buns 2 inches apart on a buttered baking sheet. Cover them and allow them to double in size.

**STEP IV.**
1 egg, at room temperature
  *mixed with*
1 teaspoon water

Using a very sharp knife or razor, cut a shallow cross into each bun. Brush them lightly with glaze.

*Powdered sugar glaze*
3/4 cup powdered sugar
1 tablespoon (or more) cream

**STEP V.**
Bake the buns at 400°F for 10 to 15 minutes. Transfer them to a cooling rack. When the buns have cooled completely, brush them with powdered sugar glaze: place powdered sugar

in a small bowl and add cream to make the desired consistency. Drizzle the powdered sugar glaze along the lines of the cross. Serve the buns with lemon curd.

Makes 1¾ cups

# Lemon Curd

**3 eggs, at room temperature**
**Grated rind and juice of 2 lemons**
**6 tablespoons unsalted butter**
**1 cup sugar**

In the top of a double boiler placed over medium heat, beat the eggs, lemon rind, and lemon juice. Add the butter and sugar and stir constantly until the butter melts and the mixture thickens. This will take about 5 minutes. Remove the pan from the heat and allow it to cool. If poured into clean, warm jars and sealed, lemon curd will keep for 2 weeks.

# QUICK BREADS

There are two kinds of quick breads, batter quick breads and dough quick breads. Batter quick breads are tea breads, muffins, corn breads, spoonbreads, or any bread made from a batter using chemical leavening. Biscuit and Irish soda breads are examples of dough quick breads. They are also chemically raised but, instead of being mixed into a moist, pourable batter, they are formed into a dough that is briefly kneaded and shaped.

Some batter breads, for example, Raised Cornmeal Squash Bread, contain yeast. Nevertheless, they are not kneaded. Gluten is developed by vigorous beating, and the dough is allowed to rise for long periods of time, as are kneaded yeast breads.

In making quick breads, you should know that:

- All-purpose flour is more appropriate than higher-gluten bread flour. Since the point is a fast rise, one wants to avoid, rather than encourage, the development of gluten.

- Embellishments added to quick breads are interchangeable if the overall quantities are kept constant.

- Except for tea breads, whose complex flavors mellow as they are allowed to ripen for several days, quick breads should be eaten as soon after baking as possible.

Because a flour without lumps accurately measured and incorporated evenly into the other dry ingredients is important for the successful outcome of quick breads, I would like to recommend Julia Child's method of measuring. Cover your work surface with a sheet of waxed paper. Place a dry-ingredient type measuring cup in the center of the paper and sift the flour directly into the cup until it overflows. Do not tap the cup or press down on the flour. Using a knife or other flat utensil, level the flour and transfer it to a mixing bowl. Fractions of cups and spoonfuls may be measured in the same manner. Due to improved milling procedures, flour does not always need to be sifted, but the method described above does ensure accurate measurements.

# CORN BREADS

Makes 1 flat 8-inch loaf

## Oats 'n' Corn Skillet Bread

*Its savory overtones are lovely with hearty soups and egg dishes.*

In a large bowl, mix the flour, oats, cornmeal, baking powder, baking soda, salt, Cheddar cheese, scallions, Parmesan cheese, and parsley well. In a separate, slightly larger bowl, beat the egg and buttermilk. Quickly stir in the dry ingredients and let the mixture stand for 15 minutes. Meanwhile, heat 2 tablespoons of vegetable oil in a 7- to 8-inch ovenproof skillet. Pour in the batter and drizzle 1 tablespoon of olive oil over the top. Bake the bread in a 400°F oven for 15 minutes or until a toothpick inserted into the center comes out clean. Serve piping hot.

### INGREDIENTS

1/2 cup unbleached all-purpose flour

3/4 cup rolled oats

1/4 cup yellow cornmeal

1 teaspoon baking powder

1/4 teaspoon baking soda

1/2 teaspoon salt

3/4 cup grated sharp Cheddar cheese

1/3 cup minced scallions

3 tablespoons freshly grated Parmesan cheese

2 tablespoons minced fresh parsley

1 egg, at room temperature

3/4 cup buttermilk

2 tablespoons vegetable oil

1 tablespoon olive oil

# Gigi's Sweet Corn Skillet Bread

## INGREDIENTS

2 tablespoons
vegetable oil

2 cups whole-wheat
flour

2 cups corn flour

1 teaspoon salt

2 tablespoons
baking powder

3 tablespoons
poppyseed

1 teaspoon
cinnamon

1/8 teaspoon
cardamom

1/2 teaspoon
freshly grated
nutmeg

2 eggs, at room
temperature

2 cups milk

1-1/4 cups fresh
corn kernels

3 tablespoons
honey

1/4 cup unsalted
butter, melted

1 cup raisins

1/2 cup chopped
almonds

*Fresh corn, raisins, almonds, and spices make a surprisingly sweet and delicious corn bread.*

Pour 2 tablespoons of vegetable oil into a 10- to 12-inch cast iron skillet and preheat it in a 375°F oven. Meanwhile, in a large bowl, combine the whole-wheat flour, corn flour, salt, baking powder, poppyseed, cinnamon, cardamom, and nutmeg. In a separate smaller bowl, beat the eggs, milk, fresh corn, honey, and butter. Stir the liquid ingredients into the dry, stirring only until the dry ingredients are moistened. Add the raisins and almonds and quickly pour the batter into the preheated skillet. Bake the bread in a 375°F oven for 35 to 40 minutes or until a toothpick inserted into the center comes out clean. Serve immediately.

# Custard Corn Bread

1 cup coarse
  ground cornmeal

1/2 cup whole-
  wheat flour

1/2 cup unbleached
  all-purpose flour

2 teaspoons baking
  powder

1/2 teaspoon salt

2 eggs, at room
  temperature

1/4 cup corn oil

1/4 cup honey

3 cups buttermilk

*Except that it calls for whole-wheat flour, this recipe is typical of moist, custard-variety corn breads.*

In a small bowl, mix the cornmeal, whole-wheat flour, unbleached all-purpose flour, baking powder, and salt thoroughly and set the mixture aside. Using a larger bowl, beat the eggs lightly. Add the corn oil, honey, and buttermilk and beat well. Slowly add the dry ingredients, stirring only until they are moistened and most of the lumps are removed. It is all right for a few lumps to remain. Pour the batter, which will be quite thin, into a buttered 7-by-11-inch baking dish and bake it at 350°F for 25 to 30 minutes, or until the top springs back when lightly touched.

---

# Corn Muffins with Blueberries

1-1/2 cups fresh
  blueberries

1 cup yellow
  cornmeal

1 cup unbleached
  all-purpose flour

1/4 cup sugar

2 teaspoons baking
  powder

1/2 teaspoon
  baking soda

3/4 teaspoon salt

1 egg, at room
  temperature

1 cup buttermilk

1/4 cup unsalted
  butter, melted

*Little bursts of blueberries mellow the crunchy texture of cornmeal.*

Wash the blueberries, drain them on a towel, and place them in a strainer. Holding the strainer over a plate, sprinkle the berries with flour and tap the strainer so that the excess flour falls through. This will help suspend the blueberries in the batter and prevent them from bleeding.

In a large bowl, combine the cornmeal, flour, sugar, baking powder, baking soda, and salt. In a separate smaller bowl, beat the egg, buttermilk, and melted butter. Add the wet ingredients to the dry, stirring only until the dry ingredients are moistened. Gently stir in the blueberries.

Spoon the batter into well-buttered or paper-lined muffin cups and bake at 400°F for 20 to 25 minutes or until a toothpick inserted into the center of a muffin comes out clean.

For more information about muffins, see page 183.

# Raised Cornmeal Squash Bread

## INGREDIENTS

**1-1/2 cups grated yellow squash**

**1 teaspoon salt**

**1/2 cup milk, scalded and cooled to lukewarm**

**1 tablespoon active dry yeast**

**2 tablespoons honey**

**1 egg, at room temperature**

**1/4 cup yellow cornmeal**

**2 tablespoons chopped fresh basil**

**1/3 cup freshly grated Parmesan cheese**

**2 tablespoons olive oil**

**1 teaspoon salt**

**3 to 3-1/2 cups unbleached all-purpose flour**

**Additional olive oil**

*Glaze*

**1 egg**
**Pinch salt**

*The longer and harder the batter is beaten, the lighter and fluffier the final texture will be.*

To prepare the squash, distribute it evenly over several layers of paper towel. Sprinkle it with 1 teaspoon of salt and place 3 folded paper towels on top of it. Allow the squash to exude moisture while you are proceeding with the recipe.

In a large bowl, beat the milk, yeast, and honey well. Cover this mixture with a warm damp towel and let it bubble for 15 to 20 minutes. Then uncover the bowl and beat in the egg, cornmeal, basil, Parmesan cheese, olive oil, 1 teaspoon of salt, and the grated squash, which has been patted dry. Add the flour, 1 cup at a time, and beat the mixture until it develops into a sticky dough. Continue beating it for about 200 strokes. (This is done in place of kneading.) Brush a little olive oil on top. Cover it and let it rise until the dough has doubled.

With an oiled spoon, stir down the dough to remove the air. Shape it into a loaf and place it in a buttered 9-by-5-by-3-inch loaf pan. Cover the pan and let the bread rise until it has reached the top edge. To prepare the glaze, beat the egg with a pinch of salt and brush this lightly over the dough. Bake the bread at 375°F for 40 to 50 minutes, or until its bottom sounds hollow when tapped. Cool the bread in its pan for 10 minutes before turning it out onto a rack to cool completely.

# Corn Muffins with Pumpkin and Toasted Pine Nuts

## INGREDIENTS

**1/2 cup pine nuts, toasted**

**1 cup unbleached all-purpose flour**

**1 cup yellow cornmeal**

**2 teaspoons baking powder**

**1/2 teaspoon baking soda**

**3/4 teaspoon salt**

**1-1/2 teaspoons pumpkin pie spice**

**1 egg at room temperature**

**1/2 cup cooked pumpkin**

**1/4 cup** *each* **honey and molasses**

**2/3 cup buttermilk**

**1/4 cup unsalted butter, melted**

*An unusual muffin filled to the brim with rich and exotic ingredients.*

Spread the nuts evenly on a baking sheet and bake them at 400°F for about 5 minutes, or until they *just begin* to turn golden. In a medium-sized bowl, mix the flour, cornmeal, baking powder, baking soda, salt, and pumpkin pie spice well. In a separate larger bowl, beat the egg lightly; add to it the pumpkin, honey, molasses, buttermilk, and melted butter and beat them well. Then add the dry ingredients, stirring just until they are moistened. Gently add the toasted pine nuts. Pour the batter into well-buttered or paper-lined muffin cups and bake at 400°F for about 15 minutes or until a toothpick inserted into the center of a muffin comes out clean.

For more information about muffins, see the introduction to the muffin section, p. 183.

# Peanut Butter Corn Sticks

*A hint of nuts delicately flavors these miniature corn-on-the-cobs.*

## INGREDIENTS

**Bacon fat**

**1 cup unbleached all-purpose flour**

**1 cup yellow or white cornmeal**

**2 teaspoons baking powder**

**1 teaspoon salt**

**1 tablespoon sugar**

**1/4 cup unsalted butter, melted**

**1/4 cup peanut butter**

**1 cup milk**

**2 eggs, at room temperature**

Heavily grease a corn stick mold with bacon fat and preheat the mold in a 425°F oven while you are preparing the batter.

For the batter, combine the flour, cornmeal, baking powder, salt, and sugar in a large bowl. Melt the butter and peanut butter in a small saucepan. In a separate smaller bowl, beat the milk and eggs and gradually stir in the melted peanut butter mixture, beating until the ingredients are well blended. Pour the liquid ingredients into the dry, stirring only until the dry ingredients are moistened. This is a lumpy batter.

Fill the preheated mold with batter and bake the sticks in a 425°F oven for 7 to 10 minutes, or until their crusts are golden and a toothpick inserted into the center of a corn-stick comes out clean. Repeat until all the batter is used.

Be sure to season your mold according to the manufacturer's instructions before using it.

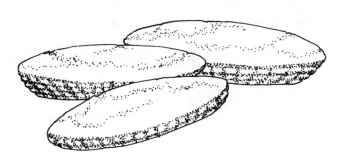

# SPOONBREADS

Often thought of as batter breads, spoonbreads are actually based on what is called a *rick* of cornmeal, butter, milk, and egg yolks into which stiffly beaten egg whites are folded. This mixture is baked until, like a soufflé, it puffs and turns golden. In consistency spoonbread falls somewhere between a soufflé and a corn bread. Its texture is more dense and less fragile than a soufflé, the proportion of rick to egg whites being greater. Its rise and its fall are much less dramatic. It is soft enough to be eaten with a spoon, or fork, unlike ordinary bread, which is sliced and usually spread with something.

Before the 19th century, spoonbreads were considered strictly a bread—just not of the sort one cuts. Its uses eventually expanded. The mild flavor of spoonbread welcomes embellishment and, since it deflates comparatively slowly, it is easy to top with a sauce or, for breakfast, fruit preserves or honey. Either as a main dish or a protein-rich side dish, spoonbreads served piping hot lend themselves to practically any home-style meal.

Spoonbreads are best with very tender centers. Do not overcook.

---

Serves 6 to 8

## Basic Spoonbread

### INGREDIENTS

**3 cups milk (you may use half and half)**

**1 cup cornmeal**

**1-1/2 teaspoons salt**

**1/2 teaspoon freshly ground pepper**

**1/3 cup unsalted butter**

**4 eggs, at room temperature, separated**

In a large, heavy-bottomed saucepan, bring the milk to a boil. Reducing the heat to low, gradually stir in the cornmeal and continue cooking, stirring constantly, until the mixture thickens. This will take about 5 minutes. Remove the pan from the heat and stir in the salt, pepper, butter, and egg yolks. Beat the egg whites until they are stiff but not dry and lightly fold them into the corn mixture.

Pour the batter into a well-buttered 2-quart baking dish and bake it at 350°F for 30 to 40 minutes or until all but the very center is set.

# Fresh Corn Spoonbread

## INGREDIENTS

- 1-1/2 cups fresh, husked corn kernels
- 3 cups buttermilk
- 2 teaspoons salt
- 1 cup yellow cornmeal
- 6 tablespoons unsalted butter
- 1/4 teaspoon freshly ground nutmeg
- 1/4 teaspoon cayenne pepper
- 1 tablespoon sugar
- 3 eggs, at room temperature, separated
- Pinch of salt

*Fresh corn nuggets quicken the corn flavor in a soft savory bread.*

Generously butter and preheat a 2-quart casserole. Meanwhile, in a heavy-bottomed saucepan over medium-high heat, stir the corn, buttermilk, and salt together until the mixture begins to steam. Gradually add the cornmeal. Reduce the heat to low and cook, stirring constantly, until the mixture thickens. This will take about 5 more minutes. Remove the pan from the heat and stir in the butter, nutmeg, cayenne pepper, sugar, and egg yolks. Beat the egg whites with a pinch of salt until they are stiff but not dry. Gently fold them into the corn mixture.

Pour the batter into the preheated casserole and bake it uncovered at 350°F for 40 to 45 minutes or until all but the very center is set.

# Cheddar Spoonbread

## INGREDIENTS

**1-1/4 cups milk**

**1-1/4 cups half and half**

**1 cup white cornmeal**

**1/4 cup unsalted butter**

**1 teaspoon salt**

**1/4 teaspoon freshly grated nutmeg**

**1/4 teaspoon cayenne pepper**

**1 cup grated farmhouse, or other sharp, white, Cheddar cheese**

**4 eggs, at room temperature, separated**

*A sharp, white, farmhouse Cheddar predominates in this protein-rich dish.*

In a large, heavy-bottomed saucepan, bring the milk and half and half to a boil. Gradually add the cornmeal, reduce the heat to low, and continue cooking, stirring constantly, until the mixture thickens. This will take about 5 minutes. Remove the pan from the heat and stir in the butter, salt, nutmeg, cayenne pepper, Cheddar cheese, and egg yolks. Beat the egg whites until they are stiff but not dry and gently fold them into the corn mixture.

Pour the batter into a well-buttered, 2-quart baking dish and bake it at 350°F for 30 to 40 minutes or until all but the very center is set.

# Rice Spoonbread

## INGREDIENTS

**1 cup water**

**1 teaspoon salt**

**1 tablespoon honey**

**1/2 cup white cornmeal**

**1 cup cooked white rice**

**1/4 cup unbleached all-purpose flour**

**1/2 cup heavy cream**

**1/2 cup milk**

**2 eggs, at room temperature, separated**

**1/4 cup unsalted butter, softened**

*An airy bread puffed with steamed rice.*

In a heavy saucepan bring the water, salt, honey, and cornmeal to a boil. Reduce the heat and cook the mixture, stirring constantly, for about 3 minutes or until the cornmeal has thickened. Meanwhile, in the top of a double boiler, combine the cooked rice, flour, cream, and milk. Heat it, stirring frequently, for about 20 minutes. Cool. Stir in the egg yolks, butter, and cornmeal mixture. Beat the egg whites until they are stiff but not dry and very gently fold them into the batter.

Pour the batter into a well-buttered, 1½-quart baking dish. Place the baking dish in a *bain marie* and bake the spoonbread at 350°F for 35 to 40 minutes or until its center is just firm.

Serves 4 to 6

# Zucchini Spoonbread

## INGREDIENTS

**1-1/2 cups milk**

**1-1/2 cups half and half**

**1-1/2 cups grated zucchini**

**1 cup white or yellow cornmeal**

**1/4 cup unsalted butter**

**1 teaspoon salt**

**5 drops hot pepper sauce**

**1/2 teaspoon dried oregano or 1-1/2 teaspoons fresh oregano, minced**

**1/2 cup freshly grated Parmesan cheese**

**3 eggs, at room temperature, separated**

*This spoonbread could be garnished with a rich tomato sauce for a combination of summer flavors.*

In a large saucepan over medium heat, bring the milk and half and half to a boil. Add the zucchini and cook the mixture for 1 minute, stirring constantly. Add the cornmeal and continue cooking and stirring until it begins to thicken. This will take about 5 minutes. Remove the pan from the heat and add the butter, salt, hot pepper sauce, oregano, and Parmesan cheese. Then stir in the egg yolks. Beat the egg whites until they are stiff but not dry. Fold a heaping spoonful of the cornmeal mixture into the egg whites. Then fold the entire egg white mixture back into the cornmeal. Do not overmix.

Pour the batter into a well-buttered, 2-quart casserole and bake it at 350°F for 35 to 40 minutes. The center of the spoonbread will be moist and creamy.

# Double-Layer Custard Spoonbread

Serves 8 to 10

## INGREDIENTS

1 cup cottage cheese

1 cup sour cream

1/4 cup honey

2 eggs, at room temperature

2 cups milk

1 cup club soda

1/2 cup corn oil

1-1/2 cups yellow cornmeal

1 cup regular breakfast farina or cream of wheat

1-1/2 teaspoons baking powder

1 teaspoon salt

*Club soda and cottage cheese transform an otherwise basic spoonbread into a pudding with a tangy corn bread top.*

In a large bowl, combine the cottage cheese, sour cream, honey, eggs, milk, club soda, and corn oil and beat them well. Add the cornmeal, farina, baking powder, and salt and again beat the entire mixture well. Cover it and let it stand at room temperature for 2 hours.

Pour the batter (it will be thin) into a well-buttered 13-by-9-by-2-inch baking dish and bake it at 375°F for 35 to 45 minutes. The baked spoonbread will have two layers: one thin and custardy; the other, a dense tangy corn bread.

# Grits "Soufflé"

Serves 4 to 6

## INGREDIENTS

1 cup quick cooking grits

4 cups boiling water

1 teaspoon salt

1/2 pound grated sharp Cheddar *or* Jarlsberg cheese

1/2 cup unsalted butter

3 eggs, at room temperature

1/3 cup milk

*Though grits are unusual in such an elegant ambiance, the light texture and cheesy flavor of the ingredients enliven and transform this southern synonym for breakfast. Indeed it makes a wonderful luncheon with a salad or soup (lentil or possibly gazpacho) or something spicy like chili.*

Combine the grits and water in a large, heavy-bottomed saucepan and cook over medium heat, stirring frequently, until very thick. This will take about 12 minutes. Stir in the salt, cheese, and butter. Beat the eggs and milk and thoroughly stir them into the grits mixture. Pour the batter into a well-buttered, 2-quart soufflé dish and bake the "soufflé" at 350°F for about 1 hour until a knife inserted into the center comes out clean.

# Indian Pudding I

## INGREDIENTS

**2 cups milk**

**3 tablespoons yellow cornmeal**

**1 tablespoon unsalted butter**

**1/2 cup light, unsulphured molasses**

**2 eggs, at room temperature**

**1/2 teaspoon salt**

**1/4 teaspoon mace**

**1/2 teaspoon cinnamon**

**1/8 teaspoon ginger**

**Heavy cream**

*Like pumpkin pie in taste and texture, a light smooth pudding that makes a marvelous and wholesome dessert.*

In a heavy-bottomed saucepan, heat the milk until it is hot but not scalded. Gradually stir in the cornmeal and continue cooking over medium heat, stirring constantly, until the mixture thickens to the consistency of a white sauce. This will take about 15 to 20 minutes. Remove the pan from the heat and stir in the butter and molasses. Gradually beat in the eggs, salt, mace, cinnamon, and ginger. Pour the batter into a buttered, 1-quart baking dish and bake it at 300°F for 1 hour and 15 to 25 minutes, or until a knife inserted into the center of the pudding just comes out clean. Cool it for at least 1 hour before serving with heavy cream.

*Variation*—stir 1 cup of cooked fresh corn kernels into the batter just before baking.

# Indian Pudding II

*A thick hearty pudding for a winter meal.*

## INGREDIENTS

**4 cups milk**

**1/4 cup bulgur wheat**

**1/4 cup yellow cornmeal**

**2 tablespoons unsalted butter**

**1/2 cup light, unsulphured molasses**

**3 tablespoons honey**

**3 eggs, at room temperature**

**1 teaspoon salt**

**1/4 teaspoon cloves**

**1/2 teaspoon cinnamon**

**1/2 teaspoon ginger**

**Heavy cream**

In a heavy-bottomed saucepan, heat the milk until it is hot but not scalded. Gradually stir in the bulgur wheat and cornmeal and continue cooking over medium heat, stirring constantly, until the mixture thickens to the consistency of a white sauce. This will take about 15 to 20 minutes. Remove the pan from the heat and stir in the butter, molasses, and honey. Gradually beat in the eggs, salt, cloves, cinnamon, and ginger. Pour the batter into a buttered, 1½-quart baking dish and bake the pudding at 300°F for about 2 hours, or until a knife inserted into the center of the pudding just comes out clean. Cool it for at least 1 hour before serving with heavy cream.

# BISCUITS

A good biscuit is crisp and flaky on the outside, rich and moist within, and need not be higher than one inch. Preparation should take about ten minutes. Use a soft flour such as cake flour, or all-purpose flour, chilled shortening that may be vegetable shortening, lard, unsalted butter, or half lard and half butter, a liquid, and absolutely fresh leavening.

White Lily flour, a self-rising flour made from soft winter wheat is especially fine for biscuits. If it is unavailable in your area, as will undoubtedly be the case if you live north of the Mason-Dixon line, it can be ordered by mail from the White Lily Foods Company, P.O. Box 871, Knoxville, TN 37901.

Lard is 100 percent animal fat. It contains no moisture. Butter, which has more flavor, is 20 percent water. For the flakiest dough therefore, all lard is preferable, though one sacrifices a rich butter taste. Some choose half lard, half butter as a compromise. Never use salted butter, which holds even more moisture, in biscuits.

Measure accurately and be aware that too much baking powder (used in some recipes to add height) will leave a chemical taste and make the biscuits dry. Sift the flour before measuring it and then again with the other ingredients to insure an even distribution and for the lightest possible dough. Cut the shortening (which must be cold yet soft enough to be readily incorporated) into the dry ingredients with a pastry blender or two knives until the mixture resembles coarse crumbs. The temperature of the fat is important. It must not melt. Flakiness and tenderness depend on fats being distributed in very thin layers between the layers of flour. When fat is cold, this is easier to achieve. In the oven, any moisture in the shortening will turn to steam, raising the crumbs into flaky layers.

Never add all the liquid at once. Using a fork, stir in only enough to moisten the ingredients and, since this can vary with each batch, be cautious. Knead the dough lightly (seven or eight times or for one minute), just until it gathers, on a floured surface. Do not handle the dough too much. Overworked dough will be tough and will not rise well. The point is to avoid developing gluten. Now, if you wish, you may refrigerate the dough. You will lose only a bit of height in the final product.

To roll out the dough, you can either use a rolling pin or pat it out to half an inch thick with your fingers. The top does not have to be perfectly smooth. If you roll the dough out to a quarter of an inch and fold it over before cutting, the finished biscuits will be easier to split. Using a floured cutter, the rim of a glass, or an ordinary cookie cutter, push *straight* down into the dough to form the shapes that you like. Do not twist the cutter. This results in a lopsided biscuit. Pull the cutter straight up and out.

Any biscuit dough can also be made into drop biscuits. These are stirred instead of kneaded just until the ingredients are moistened and then dropped onto an ungreased baking sheet.

Place the cut biscuit rounds on an ungreased baking sheet so that they almost touch, if you want soft-sided biscuits, or about an inch apart, if you want your biscuits to have crusty sides. Dough rolled thinner and cut smaller will be even crustier. Alternately, you can roll the dough out directly onto an ungreased baking sheet. Cut in into 1½-to 2-inch *squares* and move the squares about an eighth of an inch apart. For an extra brown crust, brush the tops lightly with butter before baking.

Biscuits reheat well. Wrap them in aluminum foil or in a tightly bound, wet paper bag and place the package in a 300°F oven for 10 to 12 minutes. Or, dip each biscuit quickly into hot milk and bake at 450°F for 4 minutes. You can also cut an extra pan of biscuits for later. Place the cut biscuits directly on an ungreased baking sheet, cover with waxed paper, and refrigerate the sheet. Bake the biscuits within 48 hours.

*Variations*—like bread dough, biscuit dough may be embellished by the addition of grated cheese, minced herbs, such as fresh mint, or vegetables, such as watercress, mashed fruit, such as bananas, dried fruit, such as raisins or currants, jam, grated citrus rinds, or by substituting fruit or vegetable juices for the liquid ingredient. You can also brush the top with egg white and sprinkle it with poppyseed or sesame seed just before putting the biscuits in the oven. Children like biscuits cut very small and sprinkled, before baking, with cinnamon sugar.

# Buttermilk Biscuits

## INGREDIENTS

**2 cups unbleached all-purpose flour**

**2 teaspoons baking powder**

**1/2 teaspoon baking soda**

**1/2 teaspoon salt**

**1 teaspoon sugar**

**1/3 cup unsalted butter, chilled**

**3/4 cup buttermilk**

Stir together the flour, baking powder, baking soda, salt, and sugar. Cut in the butter until the mixture resembles coarse meal. Add all but a few tablespoons of buttermilk. Mix, adding more buttermilk if necessary to develop the dough. Knead gently about 7 times. Roll or pat the dough to ½ an inch thick and cut it into rounds. Bake the biscuits at 450°F on an ungreased baking sheet for about 12 minutes.

# Sour Cream Biscuits

## INGREDIENTS

**2 cups unbleached all-purpose flour**

**2 teaspoons baking powder**

**1/2 teaspoon baking soda**

**1/2 teaspoon salt**

**1 teaspoon sugar**

**1/2 cup vegetable shortening, chilled**

**1 cup sour cream**

Stir together the flour, baking powder, baking soda, salt, and sugar. Cut the shortening into the dry ingredients until the mixture resembles coarse meal. Add the sour cream and mix well. Knead gently 7 times. Roll or pat the dough to ½ an inch thick and cut it into 2-inch rounds. Bake the biscuits at 450°F on an ungreased baking sheet for about 12 minutes.

# Whipping Cream Biscuits

*Because the cream constitutes the shortening, this is a very fast biscuit recipe to prepare.*

Stir together the flour, baking powder, salt, and sugar. Add the cream all at once and stir only until the dry ingredients are moistened. Knead the dough gently 7 times. Roll or pat it to ¾ of an inch thick and cut it into 2-inch rounds. Bake the biscuits at 450°F for 12 to 15 minutes.

### INGREDIENTS

2 cups unbleached all-purpose flour

1 tablespoon baking powder

1 teaspoon salt

2 teaspoons sugar

1 cup heavy cream

---

# Orange Biscuits

Mix the flour, baking powder, and salt in a bowl. Add the butter pieces and quickly work them into the flour until the mixture resembles coarse meal. Add ⅓ cup of milk, the orange juice, and marmalade and toss the mixture gently for 5 strokes. If more liquid is needed, add the remaining milk. Combine the dough to form a compact ball and turn it out onto a floured board. Knead gently a few times. Roll the dough ½ an inch thick and cut it into 2-inch rounds. Place the biscuits on a baking sheet. Brush them with melted butter and sprinkle them lightly with sugar. Bake the biscuits at 450°F for 10 to 14 minutes or until they are golden brown.

### INGREDIENTS

2 cups sifted unbleached all-purpose flour

2-3/4 teaspoons baking powder

1/2 teaspoon salt

1/3 cup unsalted butter, chilled and cut into small pieces

1/3 to 1/2 cup milk

1/4 cup orange juice

2 tablespoons orange marmalade

1/4 cup unsalted butter, melted

Sugar

# Very High Biscuits

## INGREDIENTS

**3 cups unbleached all-purpose flour**

**4-1/2 teaspoons baking powder**

**3/4 teaspoon cream of tartar**

**2 tablespoons sugar**

**3/4 teaspoon salt**

**3/4 cup vegetable shortening, chilled**

**1 egg, at room temperature**

**3/4 cup whole milk**

Stir together the flour, baking powder, cream of tartar, sugar, and salt. Cut the shortening into the dry ingredients until the mixture resembles coarse meal. In a separate bowl, beat the egg and milk together and add it all at once to the dry ingredients. Knead gently 7 times. Roll or pat the dough to 1 inch thick and cut it into 2-inch rounds. Bake the biscuits at 450°F on an ungreased baking sheet for about 15 minutes.

# Whole-Wheat Biscuits

## INGREDIENTS

**1-1/4 cups unbleached all-purpose flour**

**3/4 cup whole-wheat pastry flour**

**2 teaspoons baking powder**

**1/2 teaspoon baking soda**

**1/2 teaspoon salt**

**1/3 cup unsalted butter, chilled**

**1 tablespoon honey**

**3/4 cup buttermilk**

Stir together the all-purpose flour, whole-wheat pastry flour, baking powder, baking soda, and salt. Cut in the butter until the mixture resembles coarse meal. Add the honey and all but a few tablespoons of buttermilk, adding the remaining buttermilk only if it is necessary to develop a dough. Knead gently about 7 times. Roll or pat the dough ½ an inch thick and cut it into 1½-inch rounds. Bake the biscuits at 450°F on an ungreased baking sheet for about 12 minutes.

# Caraway-Cheese Biscuits

## INGREDIENTS

1-1/2 cups unbleached all-purpose flour

2 teaspoons baking powder

1/2 teaspoon baking soda

1/2 teaspoon salt

1/2 cup All-Bran

3/4 cup grated sharp Cheddar cheese

1 to 2 teaspoons caraway seed

1/3 cup vegetable shortening, chilled

3/4 cup buttermilk

Stir together the flour, baking powder, baking soda, salt, All-Bran, Cheddar cheese, and caraway seed. Cut in the shortening until the mixture resembles coarse meal. Add all but a few tablespoons of buttermilk. Mix and add more buttermilk if necessary to develop a dough. Knead gently 7 times. Roll or pat the dough ½ an inch thick and cut it into 2-inch rounds. Bake the biscuits at 450°F on an ungreased baking sheet for about 12 minutes.

# Chile-Cheese Biscuits

## INGREDIENTS

1 cup unbleached all-purpose flour

1 cup yellow cornmeal

2 teaspoons baking powder

1/2 teaspoon baking soda

1/2 teaspoon salt

1/2 cup grated Monterey Jack cheese

1/3 cup vegetable shortening, chilled

3/4 cup buttermilk

1/4 cup diced mild green chiles

*A spicy biscuit, delicious with robust fare, such as black bean soup.*

Stir together the flour, cornmeal, baking powder, baking soda, salt, and Monterey Jack cheese. Cut in the shortening until the mixture resembles coarse meal. Add the buttermilk and stir just until the dry ingredients are moistened. Add the chiles. Knead the dough gently 7 times. Roll or pat it out 1 inch thick and cut it into 2-inch rounds. Bake the biscuits on a *greased* baking sheet (or the chiles will stick) at 450°F for about 12 minutes.

# Sweet Potato-Pecan Biscuits

## INGREDIENTS

**3/4 cup cooked, mashed, unpeeled sweet potato**

**1/2 cup unsalted butter, softened**

**2 tablespoons firmly packed brown sugar**

**1/2 cup milk**

**2 cups unbleached all-purpose flour**

**1 tablespoon baking powder**

**1/2 teaspoon salt**

**1/2 cup finely chopped pecans, dusted with 1 tablespoon flour**

In a large bowl, cream the sweet potato, butter, and sugar together. Beat in the milk. In a separate smaller bowl, mix the flour, baking powder, and salt. Add the dry ingredients to the creamed mixture stirring only until the dry ingredients are moistened. Gently stir in the pecans. Knead the dough 7 times. Roll or pat it out 1 inch thick and cut it into 2-inch rounds. Bake the biscuits on a *greased* baking sheet at 375°F for 15 to 20 minutes.

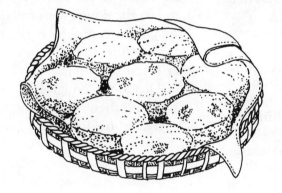

# Raised Buckwheat Biscuits

## INGREDIENTS

**2 tablespoons light, unsulphured molasses**

**2 tablespoons sugar**

**1-1/2 cups lukewarm water**

**2/3 cup milk, scalded and cooled to lukewarm**

**1 tablespoon active dry yeast**

**3-1/2 cups unbleached white bread flour**

**2 teaspoons salt**

**1/4 cup unsalted butter, melted**

**1-1/2 cups buckwheat flour**

**1-1/2 to 2-1/2 cups unbleached white bread flour**

**Unbleached flour, for rolling the biscuits in**

**3/4 cup unsalted butter, melted**

**2 egg whites, at room temperature, lightly beaten**

**1/2 cup finely chopped pecans**

*Buckwheat and a fine sprinkling of chopped pecans characterize this hearty yeasted biscuit.*

In a large bowl combine the molasses, sugar, water, milk, yeast, and 3½ cups of the white flour. Using a large spoon, whip the mixture by hand for approximately 100 strokes or until it is billowy with air bubbles. Cover the bowl with a warm, damp towel and let it rest for about 40 minutes, or until the sponge has doubled in volume.

Now whip in the salt, ¼ cup melted butter, buckwheat flour, and enough white flour to make a dough that can be kneaded. Turn it out onto a board. While kneading, add enough of the remaining flour to produce a soft dough. You may not need to use all the flour. Without cleaning the mixing bowl, butter it thoroughly. Place the dough in it face down, then turn it over and make sure that its top is completely buttered. Cover the bowl again with a damp towel and let the dough rise until it has doubled in size. Punch the dough down and let it rise again if time permits. Punch it down a final time. Knead the dough a few times and then let it rest for 5 minutes.

Divide the dough into 1½-inch balls. Roll them lightly in flour, then melted butter and arrange them on an ungreased baking sheet. Let them rise for 10 minutes.

Bake the biscuits at 400°F for 15 to 20 minutes. Remove them from the oven, brush them with beaten egg white, and sprinkle the top of each roll with chopped pecans. Place them under a broiler briefly, just long enough to cook the egg white.

# Yeasted Parmesan Biscuits

*Cheesy biscuits similar to croissants.*

## INGREDIENTS

**1-1/2 teaspoons sugar**

**1/2 cup lukewarm water**

**1/2 cup milk, scalded and cooled to luke-warm**

**1 tablespoon active dry yeast**

**1-1/2 cups unbleached white bread flour**

**1 teaspoon salt**

**1/2 cup unsalted butter, melted**

**1 cup sour cream**

**1 egg + 1 egg yolk, at room temperature**

**6 to 7 cups unbleached white bread flour**

**4 tablespoons unsalted butter, softened**

**1 egg white, at room temperature, lightly beaten**

**1 cup freshly grated Parmesan cheese**

**Caraway seed or paprika for garnish**

In a large bowl, combine the sugar, water, milk, yeast and 1½ cups of flour. Using a large spoon, whip the mixture by hand for 100 strokes or until it is billowy with air bubbles. Cover the bowl with a warm, damp towel and let the sponge rest for about 40 minutes, or until it has doubled in volume. Now whip in the salt, melted butter, sour cream, egg and egg yolk, and enough of the flour to make a dough that can be kneaded.

Turn it out onto a board. While kneading, add enough of the remaining flour to produce a smooth, limber dough. You may not need all of the flour. Without cleaning the mixing bowl, butter it thoroughly. Place the dough in it face down and let it rise until it has doubled in size. Punch the dough down and let it rise again, if time permits. Punch it down one final time. Knead it briefly and let it rest for 5 minutes.

On a floured surface, roll the dough into a 16-by-28-inch rectangle and spread it with 2 tablespoons of butter. Fold the dough into thirds, as for a business letter, then cover it and refrigerate it for 30 minutes. Now reroll the dough to a 16-by-28-inch rectangle. Spread it with the remaining 2 tablespoons of butter and fold it into thirds again. Wrap it and refrigerate it again for 30 minutes. Reroll the dough one final time ½ an inch thick.

With a 1-inch cutter cut it into rounds as closely together as possible. Dip the rounds into egg white, roll them in Parmesan cheese, and place them on a well-greased baking sheet. Sprinkle the tops with caraway seed or paprika and let them rise for 15 to 20 minutes. Do not form the remaining dough into a ball and reroll. Because of the butter layers, rerolling will not work. Leftover bits may be baked just like rounds. Serve them as appetizers. Bake the biscuits and extra pieces at 400°F for 12 to 15 minutes.

*Variation*—if you prefer a sweet biscuit, omit the Parmesan cheese and caraway seed or paprika. Cut the dough with a 1-inch cutter and dip each round in ½ a cup of melted butter. Then sprinkle it with cinnamon sugar and proceed as above.

# TEA CAKES &
# BATTER BREADS

Tea cakes, a hybrid between a bread and a cake, fall into the category of *batter quick breads*, as opposed to dough quick breads, of which biscuits are the best example. The procedure is three-fold: the wet and dry ingredients are mixed separately, the wet and dry ingredients are combined and, finally, the combination is baked. When making tea cakes or batter breads, bear in mind the following points.

**1.** Mix the wet ingredients so as to aerate them as much as possible, expanding their volume, and allowing them to act as a lightener for the bread. Butter, when used, should be allowed to come to room temperature first and then beaten until it is creamy. To *cream* butter and sugar means to beat the mixture until it is smooth, fluffy, and no longer gritty.

**2.** Sift the flour first separately and then together with the rest of the dry ingredients to be sure that they are well mixed and not lumped. Baking powder and baking soda need to be distributed evenly.

**3.** Vigorous mixing must be done while the wet and dry ingredients are still separate. Premixing to this stage is permissible as much in advance as necessary.

**4.** Since the idea in quick breads is to prevent the development of gluten, which begins in the presence of moisture, the wet and dry ingredients should be mixed quickly and stirred only until the dry ingredients are moistened. The batter does not have to be smooth.

**5.** Embellishments, too, are incorporated quickly, and the batter is scraped into a buttered and sometimes floured baking pan. Level the batter with a spatula.

**6.** Before adding raisins or dried fruit, toss them in a spoonful of flour. The flour will coat their slightly moist surface and keep them separate and suspended in the batter rather than clumping and sinking to the bottom as is their tendency.

**7.** Loaf pans may be dusted with fine dry bread crumbs, oatmeal, toasted wheat germ, and the like instead of flour.

**8.** If the batter fills more than a generous half of your loaf pan, use instead the next larger size. Or use a tin can, terracotta pot, or other container of the appropriate size.

**9.** All baking powder breads are improved by being allowed to stand at room temperature for 20 minutes before being placed in the oven. During this time, the batter will rise, very slightly, but just enough to prevent the crack down the center of the top that typically ails this kind of loaf.

**10.** Batter breads are done when a toothpick inserted into the center comes out clean. Or, if you press lightly on the middle of the loaf, it will feel firm. With some recipes, the bread will also pull away from the sides of the pan when it is done.

**11.** After removing them from the oven, cool batter breads in their pans for 15 minutes. Gently run a knife around the edge of the loaf before removing it to a rack to cool completely.

**12.** Never eat a batter bread immediately. Allow it to cool completely, then wrap it carefully or place it in an airtight container for two or preferably three days. Its flavors will mellow and the bread will be easier to slice without tearing.

**13.** Batter breads make wonderful sandwiches—including grilled sandwiches. Try them with cream cheese and avocado, Camembert, Jack, or other mild cheeses, or with peanut butter and bananas.

**14.** Tea cakes and batter breads are greatly appreciated as gifts and freeze exceptionally well.

# Glazed Lemon Loaf

## INGREDIENTS

**1/2 cup unsalted butter, softened**

**3/4 cup sugar**

**Grated rind of 1 lemon**

**2 eggs, at room temperature**

**1/4 cup fresh lemon juice**

**2 cups unbleached all-purpose flour**

**1 teaspoon baking powder**

**1 teaspoon salt**

### Glaze

**1/2 cup sugar**

**1/4 cup fresh lemon juice**

*A rich lemon cake saturated with a hot lemon glaze.*

In a large bowl, cream the butter and sugar together. Beat in the lemon rind and the eggs one at a time, then add the lemon juice and beat well. Add the flour, baking powder, and salt all at once, stirring just until they are moistened.

Pour the batter into a buttered 4½-inch-by-8½-inch loaf pan and bake it at 350°F for 45 to 55 minutes or until a toothpick inserted into the center comes out clean.

Meanwhile, prepare the glaze. Cook the sugar and fresh lemon juice in a small saucepan, stirring, until the sugar dissolves. Place the loaf on a large sheet of aluminum foil and brush it with half of the glaze. Let the glaze soak in for a few minutes and then brush it with the remaining glaze. Cool the loaf completely and allow it to mellow for several days before serving.

Makes 1 loaf of bread
and about ½ cup of
maple butter

# Maple-Macadamia Bread

*An elegant bread enhanced by a rich maple butter
spread.*

## INGREDIENTS

**1 cup unbleached
all-purpose flour**

**1 cup whole-wheat
flour**

**3/4 teaspoon salt**

**3/4 teaspoon baking
soda**

**1/2 teaspoon ginger**

**1/2 teaspoon
cinnamon**

**1/2 cup unsalted
butter, softened**

**2 tablespoons sugar**

**2 eggs, at room
temperature**

**3/4 cup real maple
syrup**

**3/4 cup buttermilk**

**1 cup coarsely
chopped
macadamia nuts**

*Maple Butter*

**2 tablespoons real
maple syrup**

**1/2 cup unsalted
butter, softened**

In a small bowl, combine the unbleached flour, whole-wheat
flour, salt, baking soda, ginger, and cinnamon and set them
aside. In a separate larger bowl, cream ½ cup butter and the
sugar. Add the eggs and ¾ cup maple syrup to the butter
mixture and beat it until it is thoroughly blended. Add the
dry ingredients alternately with the buttermilk, stirring
only until the dry ingredients are moistened. Stir in the
macadamia nuts.

Pour the batter into a buttered 9-by-5-by-3-inch loaf pan
and bake it at 350°F for 55 to 60 minutes, or until a toothpick inserted into the center of the bread comes out clean.

Before serving, prepare the maple butter. Cream the
maple syrup and the butter until they are smooth. Serve the
maple butter spread on slices of bread after the bread has
been allowed to mellow for several days.

Makes 2 loaves

# Persimmon Bread

*Dark, fruity and teeming with black walnuts.*

## INGREDIENTS

**2 cups unbleached all-purpose flour**

**2 cups whole-wheat pastry flour**

**1 tablespoon + 1 teaspoon baking soda**

**1 teaspoon salt**

**1 teaspoon mace**

**1/2 teaspoon cloves**

**4 eggs, at room temperature**

**1 cup unsalted butter, melted**

**1/4 cup honey**

**1-3/4 cups firmly packed brown sugar**

**2/3 cup bourbon**

**2 cups *very ripe* persimmons, mashed**

**2 cups coarsely chopped black walnuts**

**2 cups manooka raisins (large juicy black raisins obtainable in health food or natural food stores)**

In a large mixing bowl, combine the all-purpose flour, whole-wheat pastry flour, baking soda, salt, mace, and cloves. In a separate smaller bowl, beat the eggs. Add the butter, honey, brown sugar, bourbon, and mashed persimmons to the eggs and beat the mixture well. Add the liquid ingredients to the dry, stirring only until the dry ingredients are moistened. Gently stir in the walnuts and raisins.

Pour the batter into two well-buttered 9-by-5-by-3-inch loaf pans or, if you prefer, two 4-cup charlotte molds. Bake the breads at 350°F for 50 minutes to 1 hour or until a toothpick inserted into the center of a bread comes out clean.

# Spiced Coffee Tea Bread

*A light tea bread made with coffee and spices.*

## INGREDIENTS

**2 cups water**

**1/2 cup unsalted butter**

**2 cups sugar**

**1-1/2 cups raisins**

**3 teaspoons powdered instant coffee**

**1 teaspoon *each* cinnamon, cloves, allspice, freshly grated nutmeg**

**1/4 teaspoon salt**

**2 teaspoons baking soda**

**1 cup cold water**

**4 cups unbleached all-purpose flour**

In a large saucepan, bring 2 cups of water to a boil. Reduce the heat to medium and add butter, sugar, raisins, instant coffee, cinnamon, cloves, allspice, nutmeg, and salt. Stirring occasionally, simmer the mixture for 15 minutes. Remove the pan from the heat. Dissolve the baking soda in 1 cup of cold water and add it to the liquid mixture. Carefully add the flour to the liquid mixture, one cup at a time, stirring only until it is moistened.

Pour the batter into a buttered and floured bundt cake pan and bake it at 350°F for about 40 minutes, or until a toothpick inserted into the center comes out clean. Allow the bread to cool in the pan for 5 minutes before transferring it to a cooling rack to cool completely.

Makes 1 loaf

## INGREDIENTS

1 cup whole-wheat
pastry flour

1/4 cup unbleached
all-purpose flour

1/4 cup toasted
wheat germ

1 teaspoon baking
soda

3/4 teaspoon salt

1/2 teaspoon mace

1/2 cup unsalted
butter, softened

3/4 cup firmly
packed dark
brown sugar

1/2 teaspoon vanilla
extract

1 egg, at room
temperature

1-1/3 cups mashed
*very ripe* bananas
(those that are
almost entirely
blackened are too
ripe to eat but
have a perfectly
developed flavor
for bread)

1/4 cup buttermilk

Grated rind of 1
lemon

1 cup chopped
pecans

Wheat germ

# Buttermilk Banana Bread

*Wonderfully moist, this nourishing bread is delicately
flavored with bananas.*

In a small bowl, combine the whole-wheat pastry flour,
unbleached flour, wheat germ, baking soda, salt, and mace
and set them aside. In a separate larger bowl, cream the butter and brown sugar. Beat the vanilla and egg and then the
mashed bananas and buttermilk into the butter mixture.
Add to this the dry ingredients, stirring only until they are
moistened. Gently stir in the lemon rind and pecans.

Butter a 9-by-5-by-3-inch loaf pan and lightly dust it
with wheat germ. Pour in the batter and bake it at 350°F for
50 to 55 minutes, or until a toothpick inserted into the
center of the bread comes out clean. Cool the loaf in its pan
briefly before transferring it to a rack to cool completely.

# Carrot Bread with Hazelnuts

*A lemon-infused bread, lightly spiced and wholesome.*

## INGREDIENTS

2 cups whole-wheat pastry flour

2 teaspoons baking powder

1 teaspoon baking soda

1/2 teaspoon salt

1 teaspoon cinnamon

1/2 teaspoon freshly grated nutmeg

1/2 cup unsalted butter, softened

3/4 cup firmly packed light brown sugar

2 eggs, at room temperature

2 tablespoons honey

1 tablespoon grated orange peel

1-1/4 packed cups unpeeled, grated carrots

2/3 cup chopped hazelnuts

*Lemon infusion*

4 tablespoons fresh lemon juice

2 tablespoons sugar

In a small bowl, combine the flour, baking powder, baking soda, salt, cinnamon, and nutmeg and set them aside. In a separate larger bowl, cream the butter and brown sugar. Beat the eggs and honey into the butter mixture. Add the dry ingredients, stirring just until they are moistened, then stir in the orange peel, grated carrots, and hazelnuts.

Pour the batter into a buttered 9-by-5-by-3-inch loaf pan and bake it at 350°F for 45 to 50 minutes, or until a toothpick inserted into the center of the bread comes out clean. Cool the loaf in its pan briefly before transferring it to a rack to cool completely.

Meanwhile prepare the infusion. Heat the lemon juice and sugar until the sugar dissolves. While the bread is resting on the cooling rack, poke tiny holes into its top crust with a toothpick. Drizzle the lemon mixture directly into the holes, making sure that all of it is absorbed.

Makes 1 loaf

# Sweet Potato Bread

*Another vegetable bread, moist, sweet, and umber colored.*

## INGREDIENTS

1-1/2 cups whole-wheat pastry flour

1/2 teaspoon salt

1/4 teaspoon baking soda

1/4 teaspoon baking powder

1 teaspoon cinnamon

1/2 teaspoon allspice

1/2 cup safflower oil

1 cup firmly packed light brown sugar

1 egg, at room temperature

1 packed cup unpeeled, grated raw sweet potato

2/3 cup chopped walnuts

In a small bowl, combine the flour, salt, baking soda, baking powder, cinnamon, and allspice and set them aside. In a separate larger bowl, combine the oil and brown sugar. Using a spoon, beat the egg into the oil mixture. Add the dry ingredients, stirring only until they are moistened. Gently stir in the sweet potato and walnuts.

Pour the batter into a buttered 9-by-5-by-3-inch loaf pan and bake it at 350°F for about 50 minutes, or until a tooth-pick inserted into the center of the bread comes out clean.

# Irish "Spotted Dog" Soda Bread

INGREDIENTS

**2 cups unbleached all-purpose flour**

**1 tablespoon sugar**

**1-1/4 teaspoons baking soda**

**1/2 teaspoon salt**

**1/3 cup + 1 tablespoon unsalted butter, chilled**

**1 cup currants**

**1 egg, at room temperature**

**2/3 cup buttermilk**

**Milk for glazing**

*Brown sugar and apricots instead of white sugar and currants would provide a luscious alternative.*

In a large bowl, stir together the flour, sugar, baking soda and salt. Cut in the butter until the mixture resembles coarse meal. Stir in the currants. In a separate smaller bowl, beat the egg and buttermilk and add them to the dry ingredients. Form a ball and knead it gently a few times. Gradually ease the dough into a 6-inch mound. Place the mound in a buttered pie or cake pan or in a covered container.

Traditionally Irish soda bread is baked in a container. For a lighter loaf, you can keep the container covered initially to trap moisture, thus delaying the formation of a crust, which prevents the bread from expanding to its fullest. Later remove the lid so that the surface will brown. Since the main drawback of soda breads is that they quickly dry out, the extra moisture attained from this technique is advantageous.

Slash the top with a ¼-inch deep X, brush it with milk, and bake the loaf at 375°F for 40 to 45 minutes, or until it tests done.

*Variation*—use 1 cup whole-wheat flour and 1 cup white flour for brown soda bread.

# Sherried Pumpkin Loaf

### INGREDIENTS

- 2 cups unbleached all-purpose flour
- 2 teaspoons baking soda
- 1/2 teaspoon salt
- 1-1/2 tcaspoons cinnamon
- 1/2 teaspoon cloves
- 1 cup sugar
- 1/2 cup vegetable oil
- 2 eggs, at room temperature
- 1/2 cup cream sherry
- 1 cup cooked, mashed pumpkin
- 1 cup golden raisins
- 1/2 cup chopped dates

*Serve this fruit-filled golden bread with a good cream cheese or fresh goat cheese.*

In a large mixing bowl, combine the flour, baking soda, salt, cinnamon, and cloves. In a separate smaller bowl, mix together the sugar, oil, eggs, sherry, and pumpkin. Beat well. Add the liquid ingredients to the dry, stirring just until the dry ingredients are moistened. Gently stir in the raisins and dates and pour the batter into a well-buttered 9-by-5-by-3-inch loaf pan. Bake the bread at 325°F for 40 to 50 minutes, or until a toothpick inserted into the center of the bread comes out clean.

# Orange-Zucchini Bread

## INGREDIENTS

3 cups unbleached all-purpose flour

1 teaspoon salt

1 teaspoon baking soda

1/2 teaspoon baking powder

1-1/2 teaspoons cinnamon

1 cup walnut oil

2 cups sugar

2 eggs, at room temperature

1 teaspoon vanilla extract

1 tablespoon grated orange peel

2 packed cups grated zucchini

3/4 cup chopped dates

3/4 cup chopped walnuts

*Glaze*

1/2 cup sugar

1/4 cup fresh orange juice

*Nuts and vegetables and fruit yield a nutritious dessert bread.*

In a medium-sized mixing bowl, combine the flour, salt, baking soda, baking powder, and cinnamon. Mix them well and set the bowl aside. In a separate larger bowl, beat the oil, sugar, eggs, vanilla, and orange peel. Using a spoon, add the dry ingredients, stirring just until they are moistened. Gently stir in the zucchini, dates, and walnuts.

Pour the batter into 2 buttered 4½-by-8½-inch loaf pans and bake the breads at 350°F for 55 to 60 minutes or until a toothpick inserted into the center of a bread comes out clean.

Meanwhile prepare the glaze. Combine the sugar and fresh orange juice in a small saucepan and heat them until the sugar dissolves. When the loaves are done, cool them in their pans briefly, then turn them out onto a large sheet of aluminum foil. Brush the loaves with half the glaze and let it soak in. Then brush them with the remaining glaze. Be sure to retrieve any glaze that may have spilled onto the foil and, when all the glaze has been absorbed, transfer the loaves to a cooling rack.

# GINGERBREAD*

Makes 1 loaf, 8
inches square

## Bread Gingerbread

*Old World gingerbreads like this one are presented during instead of after a meal.*

INGREDIENTS

1 cup unbleached
all-purpose flour

1/2 cup whole-
wheat flour

1/2 teaspoon *each*
baking powder
and baking soda

1/4 teaspoon salt

1 teaspoon
cinnamon

1 teaspoon ginger

1/4 teaspoon cloves

1/4 cup unsalted
butter, softened

1/2 cup firmly
packed light
brown sugar

1/2 cup light,
unsulphured
molasses

1 egg, at room
temperature

In a small bowl, combine the all-purpose flour, whole-wheat flour, baking powder, baking soda, salt, cinnamon, ginger, and cloves. Mix them well and set the mixture aside. In a separate larger bowl, cream the butter and sugar. Beat in the molasses and egg. Gradually add the dry ingredients, stirring only until they are moistened.

Pour the batter into a buttered 8-inch square baking pan and bake the bread at 325°F for 25 to 30 minutes or until a toothpick inserted into its center comes out clean. Serve the gingerbread with sweet butter. Lemon curd also goes nicely with this bread. See page 142 for a recipe.

*The following gingerbread recipes call for dried ginger. If you wish to substitute finely minced fresh ginger, you will need at least three times as much, or to taste.

# Ginger Beer Bread

*Crystallized ginger delicately flavors this heady
gingerbread.*

INGREDIENTS

1/2 cup unsalted
 butter, softened

2 tablespoons
 firmly packed
 light brown sugar

1 egg, at room
 temperature

1 cup light,
 unsulphured
 molasses

1 cup dark beer, at
 room temperature

2-1/4 cups sifted
 all-purpose flour

1 teaspoon baking
 soda

1/2 teaspoon salt

1 teaspoon
 cinnamon

1/4 teaspoon
 allspice

3 tablespoons finely
 chopped crystal-
 lized ginger

Whipped cream,
 for garnish

Additional crystal-
 lized ginger, finely
 chopped, for
 garnish

In a large bowl, cream the butter and brown sugar. Beat in
the egg, molasses, and beer. In a separate smaller bowl, combine the flour, baking soda, salt, cinnamon, and allspice.
Add these to the creamed mixture and stir in the ginger.

Pour the batter into a buttered and floured 9-by-9-by-2-
inch baking pan and bake the gingerbread at 325°F for 50
to 60 minutes or until a toothpick inserted into its center
comes out clean. Serve the gingerbread with whipped cream
and a sprinkling of additional crystallized ginger.

## INGREDIENTS

**1-1/4 cups fresh blueberries**

**1 tablespoon all-purpose flour**

**1-3/4 cups unbleached all-purpose flour**

**1 teaspoon baking soda**

**1/4 teaspoon salt**

**1 teaspoon ginger**

**2 teaspoons cinnamon**

**1/4 teaspoon allspice**

**1/4 cup unsalted butter, softened**

**1/2 cup firmly packed light brown sugar**

**2 eggs, at room temperature**

**1/2 cup sour cream**

**1/2 cup light, unsulphured molasses**

**Powdered sugar**

**Whipped cream**

# Gingerbread with Blueberries

*An unexpected but exquisite combination to celebrate the fresh blueberry season.*

Wash the fresh berries, drain them on a towel, and place them in a strainer. Holding the strainer over a plate, sprinkle the berries with flour and tap the strainer so that the excess flour falls through. This will help suspend the berries in the batter and prevent them from bleeding.

In a small bowl, combine the flour, baking soda, salt, ginger, cinnamon, and allspice and set the mixture aside. In a separate larger bowl, cream the butter and sugar. Beat the eggs, sour cream, and molasses into the butter mixture. Using a spoon, add the dry ingredients, stirring only until they are moistened. Gently fold in the blueberries.

Pour the batter into a buttered, 8-inch square baking pan and bake the gingerbread at 350°F for 40 to 50 minutes, or until a toothpick inserted into its center comes out clean. When the gingerbread has cooled completely, dust it decoratively with powdered sugar and serve it with whipped cream.

INGREDIENTS

**2 cups unbleached
all-purpose flour**

**1 teaspoon baking
soda**

**1/2 teaspoon salt**

**2 teaspoons ginger**

**1 teaspoon
cinnamon**

**1/2 teaspoon
freshly grated
nutmeg**

**1/2 teaspoon
allspice**

**1/2 cup unsalted
butter, softened**

**1/2 cup firmly
packed light
brown sugar**

**2 eggs, at room
temperature,
separated**

**3/4 cup sour cream**

**1/2 cup light,
unsulphured
molasses**

**1 cup manooka
raisins (plump and
juicy black raisins
to be found in
health food and
natural food
stores)**

**2 tablespoons dark
rum**

**Pinch of cream of
tartar**

**2 tablespoons sugar**

**Sifted powdered
sugar**

*Glaze*

**1/2 cup apple jelly**

**1 tablespoon dark
rum**

# Rum-Raisin Gingerbread

*With a tangy rum-flavored apple-jelly glaze.*

In a small bowl, combine the flour, baking soda, salt, ginger, cinnamon, nutmeg, and allspice and set the mixture aside. In a separate larger bowl, cream the butter and brown sugar. Beat the egg yolks first, then the sour cream, into the butter and sugar mixture until they are thoroughly amalgamated and then beat in the molasses, raisins, and rum.

Using a spoon, stir the dry ingredients into the creamed mixture until the two are just combined. In a separate bowl, beat the egg whites until they are foamy. Add the cream of tartar and continue beating until they form soft peaks. Add 2 tablespoons of sugar and continue beating the egg whites until they are stiff but not dry. Fold a large spoonful of the cake batter into the egg whites. Then fold the egg white mixture back into the cake batter. *Do not overmix.*

Spoon the batter into a buttered, 9-inch square baking pan and bake the gingerbread at 350°F for 40 to 45 minutes, or until a toothpick inserted into the center comes out clean. Cool the gingerbread in its pan for 10 minutes. Remove it from the pan and cool it for an additional 10 minutes on a cooling rack.

While it is cooling, prepare the glaze. Combine the apple jelly and rum in a small saucepan. Cook them over low heat, stirring occasionally, until the jelly melts and the mixture is smooth. Brush this glaze over the warm cake and let it cool completely. Before serving, use a decorative stencil and sprinkle the cake lightly with powdered sugar.

# Gingerbread Men

*These cookies are highly scented, puffy, and soft.*

## INGREDIENTS

**1 cup unsalted
butter, softened**

**1 cup firmly
packed light
brown sugar**

**1 egg, at room
temperature**

**1 cup light,
unsulphured
molasses**

**2 tablespoons cider
vinegar**

**5 cups unbleached
all-purpose flour**

**1-1/2 teaspoons
baking soda**

**1/2 teaspoon salt**

**2 teaspoons ginger**

**1-1/4 teaspoons
cinnamon**

**1 teaspoon cloves**

**Raisins and red
hots for decoration**

In a large bowl, cream the butter and brown sugar until the mixture is light and fluffy. Add the egg, molasses, and vinegar and beat well. In a separate smaller bowl, combine the flour, baking soda, salt, ginger, cinnamon, and cloves. Add these to the creamed mixture, about 1 cup at a time, beating well after each addition. Divide the dough into 4 portions, dust each with flour and wrap it in waxed paper. Flatten each portion slightly before refrigerating it for at least 3 hours or overnight.

Remove the portions from the refrigerator one at a time. Place a fresh piece of waxed paper large enough to cover a baking sheet on a flat surface and flour it liberally. Working quickly, roll one portion of dough ¼ of an inch thick. Cut it with a floured gingerbread man cutter and decorate each man with raisins and red hots. Remove the dough from *around* the cut shapes. (This scrap dough may be rechilled, so that it doesn't stick, and then rerolled.) Rolled out cookies retain their shapes better if they are not disturbed after cutting, so lift the entire piece of waxed paper holding all the cut out and decorated men and place it directly onto a baking sheet.

Repeat this process for the other 3 portions of dough and bake the men at 375°F for 8 to 10 minutes or until a light finger imprint no longer remains on the cookie. Transfer the cookies to a rack to cool. If stored properly, the gingerbread men will stay fresh for at least 10 days.

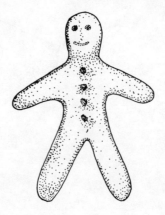

# MUFFINS

Strictly speaking, muffins are made according to a precise formula. This calls for oil (or a melted solid shortening) and a flour to liquid ratio of 2:1. The dry ingredients are sifted together in one bowl, the liquid ingredients in another, and then the two are rapidly combined and spooned into muffin cups. Though many muffin recipes abide by these traditions, the strict definition has relaxed and *muffin* has come to mean almost any bread or cake baked in a muffin shape.

Interestingly, from the midst of this very loose terminology, yet another formula for a sweeter, richer, more cakelike muffin has emerged, for which a larger quantity of shortening (always solid) and sugar are creamed together before being added to the other ingredients. The texture of this muffin is finer, the keeping qualities are better and, although they are slightly more time consuming to make, there is little danger of over mixing because the extra sugar and fat naturally inhibit gluten development. This batter, in fact, *should* be beaten thoroughly. Farmhouse Cheddar Muffins are an example of this modern cakelike type.

When correctly mixed, a muffin expands to a rounded dome and has a slightly coarse, but not a crumbly, texture. To achieve this, the following instructions will be helpful.

**1.** Muffin batter is made in three steps:
   (1) The wet ingredients are mixed together
   (2) The dry ingredients are mixed together
   (3) The mixtures from steps 1 and 2 are combined

The methods used in steps 1 and 2, primarily mixing steps, are very different from that used in step 3 for combining. This distinction is crucial and must be observed.

**2.** In steps 1 and 2 be thorough. Beat the liquid ingredients together and sift and stir the dry ingredients. Make sure that the components of each mixture are completely amalgamated. For convenience, these two steps can be done as much ahead of time as necessary.

**3.** In the third step, a combining process, be spare in your movements. The aim is to combine the ingredients with the minimum of stirring (no more than fifteen to twenty strokes), developing the gluten in the flour just enough for it to trap the carbon dioxide and hold the muffins together. Do not feel compelled to mash every tiny lump or even wet every bit of unmoistened flour. When you spoon it into cups, it should not fall in ribbons (like cake batter) but in blobs. The lumps will disappear during baking and stray flakes of flour will jell. Overcombining develops the gluten too much and results in a tough muffin. Knobs or peaks on top of your muffins or long narrow holes inside usually mean the batter has been stirred too long.

**4.** The technique of forming a well in the center of the dry ingredients into which the liquid is poured makes the combining process easier.

**5.** Once the liquid and dry ingredients are combined, allow the batter to rest for several minutes to condition the ingredients and allow the leaveners to become active.

**6.** Care should be taken even when spooning the batter into the muffin cups. Rough handling at this point can deflate the batter, stretch the gluten, and result in a overly tough muffin.

**7.** Using an ice-cream scoop, if you have one, otherwise a spoon, fill very well greased or paper-lined muffin cups two-thirds full. Small muffin pans or bundt muffin pans are also suitable; be sure to adjust baking times. Fill any empty cups with water for even heat distribution and as a precaution against the muffins scorching.

**8.** Bake muffins on one shelf at a time in the middle of a preheated oven.

**9.** Test the muffins for doneness with a toothpick inserted into the center. Muffins have baked enough when the toothpick comes out clean, that is, free from moist particles of batter.

**10.** Let the muffins cool in their tins for three or four minutes, or until they shrink slightly from the sides of each cup. Gently encircle their edges with a knife and remove them to a cooling rack.

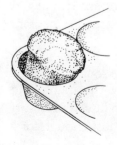

**11.** Though best eaten when freshly made, muffins may be rewarmed and, if tipped on their sides back into the muffin cups, a position that allows moisture to become trapped underneath, they will remain moist.

# Cinnamon-Pecan Muffins

## INGREDIENTS

**2 cups sifted unbleached all-purpose flour**

**2 teaspoons baking powder**

**1/2 teaspoon salt**

**2 teaspoons cinnamon**

**1/2 teaspoon freshly grated nutmeg**

**1/4 cup unsalted butter, melted**

**1/2 cup firmly packed light brown sugar**

**1 egg, at room temperature, lightly beaten**

**1 cup milk**

**1 cup coarsely chopped pecans**

In a large bowl, combine the flour, baking powder, salt, cinnamon, and nutmeg. In a separate smaller bowl, mix the melted butter, brown sugar, egg, and milk. Add the liquid ingredients to the dry, stirring only until the dry ingredients are moistened. Gently add the pecans. Spoon the batter into well-buttered or paper-lined muffin cups and bake at 425°F for about 20 minutes or until a toothpick inserted into the center of a muffin comes out clean.

# Maple-Hazelnut Muffins

## INGREDIENTS

1 cup unbleached
  all-purpose flour

1 cup bran flakes

1 teaspoon baking
  soda

1/2 teaspoon salt

2 eggs, at room
  temperature

1/2 cup sour cream

1 cup real maple
  syrup

3/4 cup coarsely
  chopped hazelnuts

### Glaze

1/2 cup real maple
  syrup

1/4 cup unsalted
  butter

*An elegant muffin for an elegant occasion.*

In a large bowl, combine the flour, bran flakes, baking soda, and salt. In a separate smaller bowl, beat the eggs. Add the sour cream and 1 cup of maple syrup and beat well. Add the liquid ingredients to the dry, stirring only until the dry ingredients are moistened. Gently stir in the hazelnuts.

Spoon the batter into well-buttered or paper-lined muffin cups and bake at 400°F for about 15 minutes, or until a toothpick inserted in the center of a muffin comes out clean.

Meanwhile prepare the glaze. In a small saucepan, heat ½ cup of maple syrup with butter until the butter melts. Remove the pan from the heat and set it aside. When the muffins are done, pierce the top of each one several times with a toothpick and drizzle 1 tablespoon of glaze into the perforations.

# Oatmeal-Raisin Muffins

## INGREDIENTS

**1-1/4 cups buttermilk**

**1-1/4 cups rolled oats**

**2 eggs, at room temperature**

**3/4 cup firmly packed dark brown sugar**

**1/2 cup unsalted butter, melted**

**1 cup unbleached all-purpose flour**

**1-1/4 teaspoons baking powder**

**1/2 teaspoon baking soda**

**1/2 teaspoon salt**

**1-1/4 cups raisins**

In a large bowl, combine the buttermilk and oats and let them stand for 1 hour. Add the eggs, brown sugar, and melted butter and beat well. In a separate smaller bowl, stir together the flour, baking powder, baking soda, and salt. Add these to the liquid ingredients, stirring only until the dry ingredients are moistened. Stir in the raisins.

Spoon the batter into well-buttered or paper-lined muffin cups and bake at 400°F for 15 minutes or until a toothpick inserted into the center of a muffin comes out clean.

# Bran Muffins I

*A light muffin having a sweet, orangy nature.*

## INGREDIENTS

- 1 cup buttermilk
- 1 cup bran flakes
- 1/4 cup unsalted butter, melted
- 1 egg, at room temperature
- 1/3 cup real maple sryup
- 1 cup unbleached all-purpose flour
- 2 teaspoons baking powder
- 1/2 teaspoon baking soda
- 1/4 teaspoon salt
- 1 tablespoon grated orange rind
- 3/4 cup golden raisins

In a large bowl, combine the buttermilk and bran flakes and let this mixture stand for 5 minutes. Gradually beat in the melted butter, egg, and maple syrup. In a separate smaller bowl, combine the flour, baking powder, baking soda, and salt. Add the dry ingredients to the liquid ingredients, stirring only until the dry ingredients are moistened. Stir in the orange rind and raisins. Spoon the batter into well-buttered or paper-lined muffin cups and bake at 375°F for 15 to 20 minutes or until a toothpick inserted into the center of a muffin comes out clean.

# Bran Muffins II

*This is a meal-in-a-muffin. Keep a jar of the batter refrigerated for fresh muffins at will.*

## INGREDIENTS

1 cup boiling water

1/2 cup vegetable oil

2-1/2 teaspoons baking soda

1 cup buttermilk

1 cup firmly packed brown sugar

2 eggs, at room temperature

1-1/2 cups unbleached all-purpose flour or 3/4 cup whole-wheat flour and 3/4 cup unbleached all-purpose flour

1 cup bran flakes

1 cup All-Bran

1 cup wheat germ

1/2 teaspoon salt

1 cup raisins

1 cup chopped walnuts

In a large bowl, combine the boiling water, oil, and baking soda and let the mixture stand until it becomes lukewarm. Beat in the buttermilk, brown sugar, and eggs. In a separate smaller bowl, mix the flour, bran flakes, All-Bran, wheat germ, and salt. Add them to the liquid ingredients, stirring only until the dry ingredients are moistened. Gently add the raisins and walnuts. Before baking, let the batter stand in the refrigerator for at least 2 hours. You may also keep this batter, well covered, in the refrigerator for up to 2 weeks.

Spoon the batter into well-buttered or paper-lined muffin cups and bake at 375°F for 20 to 25 minutes, or until a toothpick inserted into the center of a muffin comes out clean.

# Blueberry Muffins

## INGREDIENTS

- **1 cup fresh blueberries**
- **1 tablespoon all-purpose flour**
- **2 cups unbleached all-purpose flour**
- **1 teaspoon baking powder**
- **1/2 teaspoon baking soda**
- **1/2 teaspoon salt**
- **1/2 cup sugar**
- **1 cup yogurt**
- **1 egg, at room temperature, lightly beaten**
- **1/4 cup unsalted butter, melted**
- **1 teaspoon grated lemon rind**

Wash the fresh berries, drain them on a towel, and place them in a strainer. Holding the strainer over a plate, sprinkle the berries with flour and tap the strainer so that the excess flour falls through. This will help suspend the berries in the batter and prevent them from bleeding.

In a large bowl, combine the flour, baking powder, baking soda, salt, and sugar. In a separate smaller bowl, mix the yogurt, egg, melted butter, and lemon rind. Add the liquid ingredients to the dry, stirring only until the dry ingredients are moistened. Gently stir in the blueberries. Spoon the batter into well-buttered or paper-lined muffin cups and bake at 350°F for 15 to 20 minutes or until a toothpick inserted into the center of a muffin comes out clean.

# Banana-Blueberry Muffins

*Bananas and lemon perfectly set off the flavor and texture of blueberries.*

## INGREDIENTS

- 1-1/4 cup fresh blueberries
- 1 tablespoon all-purpose flour
- 2 cups sifted unbleached all-purpose flour
- 1 teaspoon baking powder
- 1 teaspoon baking soda
- 3/4 teaspoon salt
- 1/3 cup firmly packed light brown sugar
- 1 egg, at room temperature
- 1/2 cup buttermilk
- 1/4 cup unsalted butter, melted
- 1 mashed, very ripe banana
- 1 teaspoon vanilla extract
- 1 teaspoon grated lemon rind

Wash the fresh berries, drain them on a towel, and place them in a strainer. Holding the strainer over a plate, sprinkle the berries with flour and tap the strainer so that the excess flour falls through. This will help suspend the berries in the batter and prevent them from bleeding.

In a large bowl, combine the flour, baking powder, baking soda, salt, and brown sugar. In a separate smaller bowl, beat the egg. Add the buttermilk, butter, mashed banana, and vanilla to the egg and beat well. Add the liquid ingredients to the dry, stirring only until the dry ingredients are moistened. Gently stir in the blueberries and lemon rind.

Spoon the batter into well-buttered or paper-lined muffin cups and bake the muffins at 400°F for 20 to 25 minutes, or until a toothpick inserted into the center of a muffin comes out clean.

# Cranberry Upside-Down Muffins

INGREDIENTS

1-1/2 cups fresh
  cranberries

3/4 cup sugar

1 tablespoon water

1/2 teaspoon
  freshly grated
  nutmeg

1 tablespoon grated
  orange rind

2 cups unbleached
  all-purpose flour

1 tablespoon baking
powder

1/2 teaspoon salt

1/3 cup sugar

1 egg, at room
  temperature

1/4 cup unsalted
  butter, melted

1 cup milk

*Begin the cranberry season with these lovely scarlet jewels. A sparkling addition to a holiday dinner.*

Place the cranberries, ¾ cup sugar, water, nutmeg, and orange rind in a heavy-bottomed saucepan and cook them over medium heat, stirring frequently (so that the sugar does not stick to the bottom of the pan) until the sugar dissolves and the berries pop open; about 10 minutes. Remove the pan from the heat and set it aside.

In a large mixing bowl, combine the flour, baking powder, salt, and ⅓ cup sugar. In a separate smaller bowl, beat the egg, butter, and milk. Add the liquid ingredients to the dry, stirring only until the dry ingredients are moistened.

Divide the cranberry mixture among 12 well-buttered muffin cups and gently spoon the batter over it. Bake the muffins at 400°F for 15 to 20 minutes or until a toothpick inserted into the center of a muffin comes out clean. Let the muffins cool in their cups for 2 minutes, then invert them onto cooling racks so that the cranberry topping shows.

# Orange-Date-Nut Muffins

## INGREDIENTS

**1 cup whole-wheat flour**

**1 cup unbleached all-purpose flour**

**1/2 cup firmly packed dark brown sugar**

**2 teaspoons baking powder**

**1/2 teaspoon baking soda**

**1/2 teaspoon salt**

**1/3 cup fresh orange juice**

**2/3 cup buttermilk**

**1/4 cup unsalted butter, melted**

**1 egg, at room temperature**

**2 teaspoons grated orange rind**

**2/3 cup chopped dates (see note)**

**2/3 cup chopped walnuts**

**2 tablespoons sugar** *(optional)*

**1/2 teaspoon cinnamon** *(optional)*

In a large bowl, combine the whole-wheat flour, all-purpose flour, brown sugar, baking powder, baking soda, and salt. In a separate smaller bowl, beat the orange juice, buttermilk, butter, and egg. Add the liquid ingredients to the dry, stirring only until the dry ingredients are moistened. Gently add the orange rind, dates, and walnuts. Spoon the batter into well-buttered or paper-lined muffin cups. If you desire a topping, combine the sugar and cinnamon and sprinkle a little on top of the batter in each cup. Bake the muffins at 400°F for 15 to 20 minutes or until a toothpick inserted into the center of a muffin comes out clean.

*Note:* Avoid packaged, chopped dates that have been rolled in granulated sugar and consequently are too sweet. Instead, freeze whole dates until they are firm and chop them by hand or in a food processor. If you are using a food processor, combine the sugar in the recipe with the whole dates before chopping them, to prevent the dates from sticking together.

# Farmhouse Cheddar Muffins

INGREDIENTS

1/4 cup unsalted butter, melted

1/2 cup firmly packed dark brown sugar

1 teaspoon vanilla extract

1 egg, at room temperature

3/4 cup apple cider

1-1/4 cups unbleached all-purpose flour

3/4 cup rolled oats

1 tablespoon baking powder

1/2 teaspoon salt

1 teaspoon cinnamon

1/2 teaspoon freshly grated nutmeg

1 large pippin apple, peeled, cored, and coarsely chopped

3/4 cup diced English Farmhouse Cheddar, Caerphilly, or other very sharp Cheddar cheese

1/2 cup coarsely chopped walnuts

*Bits of apple, chopped walnuts, and cider make this muffin mildly sweet. Chunks of sharp Farmhouse Cheddar add a surprising contrast.*

In a small bowl, combine the butter, brown sugar, vanilla, egg, and cider. In a larger bowl, stir together the flour, oats, baking powder, salt, cinnamon, and nutmeg. Add the apple, cheese, and walnuts. Pour in the liquid mixture and stir only until the dry ingredients are moistened.

Spoon the batter into well-buttered or paper-lined muffin cups. Bake the muffins at 375°F for about 25 minutes, or until a toothpick inserted into the center of a muffin comes out clean.

# LEFTOVER BREAD

## Melba Toast

INGREDIENTS

**1 loaf unsliced bread; consider cheese bread, whole-wheat, oatmeal, and so on**

*This is not a lot of trouble and homemade toast is so much better than store-bought crackers.*

Freeze the loaf of bread until it is firm but may still be sliced. Remove the crusts and cut it into paper-thin slices. Bake the slices on an ungreased baking sheet at 300°F for 30 to 40 minutes, or until they are completely crisp and lightly browned.

If you are baking bread especially for melba toast, use a round or oval *pain de mie* pan, a pullman pan, or a rectangular loaf pan with a cookie sheet and weight placed over it. The lid will give the bread an even shape and a soft crumb with a dense, compact texture. There will be almost no crust, which is perfect for melba toast.

## Sesame Toasts

INGREDIENTS

**3/4 cup unsalted butter**

**2 teaspoons sesame oil**

**1 egg, at room temperature, lightly beaten**

**1/2 teaspoon salt**

**2 baguettes, cut at an angle into 1/2-inch slices**

**1/2 cup sesame seeds**

*Toasts alone are excellent appetizers. They also can be served with cheese or pâté.*

In a small saucepan, melt the butter and sesame oil together. Mix the egg with salt. Brush the baguette slices on one side only, first with butter, then with egg, and arrange them on an ungreased baking sheet. Sprinkle the slices lightly with sesame seeds and bake them at 375°F for 20 minutes, or until they turn crisp and golden.

# Butter Croutons

INGREDIENTS

**2-1/2 cups cubed egg bread**

**1/2 cup clarified butter**

To make clarified butter, melt ¾ cup butter in a small saucepan. Skim off the milky foam from the top and then cautiously pour off the clear yellow liquefied butter into a clean container, being careful to leave behind the dregs in the bottom of the saucepan. Sauté the bread and clarified butter together in a heavy-bottomed skillet, stirring frequently until the bread cubes are crisp and light.

# Garlic Croutons

INGREDIENTS

**3 cloves garlic, crushed**

**2 tablespoons vegetable oil**

**Fresh basil or oregano to taste** *(optional)*

**4 slices bread**

*Instead of cubes, use fancy aspic or jelly cutters or, for a larger hors d'oeuvre size, use cookie cutters and more slices of bread. A bag of these small fancy croutons makes a lovely gift.*

In a blender, or with a mortar and pestle, blend the garlic and oil thoroughly. If desired, add the basil or oregano. Brush both sides of all 4 slices of bread with this mixture and cut them into cubes. Spread the cubes on a baking sheet and bake them at 300°F for 20 minutes. Turn them once after 10 minutes. When done, the cubes will be crisp and golden.

# Breadcrumb Cups

## INGREDIENTS

**5 slices egg bread, made into fine crumbs**

**1/4 cup unsalted butter, melted**

**1/4 teaspoon salt**

**1/2 teaspoon sage**

**1/4 teaspoon freshly ground pepper**

**1 egg white, at room temperature, lightly beaten**

*Breadcrumb cups are excellent filled with baked eggs, leftover vegetables topped with cheese, vegetable custards, or creamed diced meats.*

To make breadcrumbs, tear the bread slices in small pieces and bake them on a baking sheet in a 325°F oven for 10 to 15 minutes, stirring them occasionally. Transfer the toasted pieces to a food processor and process them into fine crumbs. If you do not have a food processor, place the toasted pieces between two sheets of aluminum foil and crimp the edges firmly. Using a rolling pin, roll the pieces until they are finely ground.

In a bowl, combine the breadcrumbs, butter, salt, sage, pepper, and egg white. Generously butter 6 muffin cups. Divide the crumb mixture evenly among them, pressing firmly on the bottoms and making sure that the crumbs reach all the way up the sides of the cups. Bake the bread cups at 350°F for 10 to 15 minutes, or until they are firm, but do not brown them any more. Carefully remove the bread cups by running a knife around their outer edge. They may be made up to one week ahead and refrigerated. Warm them again slightly before using.

Serves 4 to 6

# Grilled Almond Bread

### INGREDIENTS

**16 slices egg bread**

**1/4 cup slivered almonds**

**3 ounces almond paste**

**2 ounces cream cheese**

**3 eggs, at room temperature**

**1 cup milk**

**1/2 teaspoon vanilla extract**

**1 to 2 tablespoons vegetable oil**

*These are puffy, creamy, grilled sandwiches, elegant and easy to make.*

Tear half of the bread slices into pieces, combine them with the slivered almonds, and blend or process both together until everything is finely ground. Set the mixture aside. Blend the almond paste with the cream cheese and set it aside. Beat the eggs, milk, and vanilla. Spread the almond-cheese mixture evenly on 4 slices of bread, top them with the remaining 4 slices and cut the sandwiches diagonally.

Heat the oil in a skillet to medium. Dip each sandwich first into the egg mixture, then into the crumbs, and then again into the egg mixture. Fry the sandwiches for about 3 minutes on each side, or until they are heated through and golden brown.

*Variation*—substitute apple butter for almond paste and serve the bread with slices of apple that have been caramelized by being browned in butter and sugar.

Serves 3 to 4

# French Toast with Hazelnuts

## INGREDIENTS

**1/2 cup skinned hazelnuts**

**1/3 cup sour cream**

**2 eggs, at room temperature**

**1/4 cup Frangelico (hazelnut liqueur)**

**Butter**

**8 slices egg bread**

**Sifted powdered sugar**

**Real maple syrup, heated**

*A Frangelico, egg, and sour cream batter coat the hot nutty slices.*

Bake the shelled nuts on a large baking sheet at 350°F for 15 minutes. Rub the nuts carefully with a towel. Discard the skins and chop the nuts finely. In a small bowl beat the sour cream, eggs, and Frangelico. Heat the butter on a griddle until it is hot, but do not allow it to burn. Soak the slices of bread in the egg batter and fry them for a few minutes on each side until they are well browned. (Try to use all the batter.) Cut each piece on the diagonal and arrange the triangles attractively on a serving platter. Top with sifted powdered sugar and chopped hazelnuts and serve with a pitcher of heated maple syrup.

# Egg Bread Pudding

## INGREDIENTS

1 tablespoon
  unsalted butter,
  melted

2 tablespoons sugar

12 half-inch-thick
  slices egg or
  oatmeal bread

1/2 cup unsalted
  butter, melted

1 cup raisins

12 eggs, at room
  temperature

1 vanilla bean

3/4 cup + 2
  tablespoons sugar

Pinch of salt

4 cups milk

2 tablespoons
  bourbon (optional)

Powdered sugar

Heavy cream

*Deluxe French toast in a light vanilla custard. A spectacular egg dish for a large gathering.*

Brush the bottom and sides of a 13-by-9-by-2-inch baking dish with 1 tablespoon of melted butter. Sprinkle it evenly with 2 tablespoons of sugar and set the dish aside. Dip one side of each slice of bread in melted butter and arrange the slices buttered-side down in a single layer over the sugar. Sprinkle the raisins on top.

For the custard, beat the eggs in a bowl. Split a vanilla bean lengthwise and scrape the tiny seeds into the beaten eggs. Add the sugar, and a pinch of salt, and slowly beat in the milk and, if desired, the bourbon. Pour the custard over the bread slices pressing on the bread so that it absorbs as much as possible.

Place the baking dish in a *bain marie* and bake it at 325°F for 45 to 50 minutes, or until a knife inserted into the center of the pudding comes out clean. Cool the pudding on a rack until it is tepid. Just before serving, dust it with powdered sugar and serve it either topped with or accompanied by whipped cream.

# Raisin-Cranberry Stuffing

## INGREDIENTS

1-1/2 cups fresh, coarsely chopped cranberries

1/4 cup sugar

2 tablespoons grated orange peel

1 teaspoon salt

1/2 teaspoon cinnamon

6 to 7 cups toasted raisin bread, cut into cubes

2 eggs, at room temperature

1/2 cup fresh orange juice

*Raisins and oranges, cinnamon and cranberries saturate this fruit-filled stuffing.*

In a large bowl, carefully mix the cranberries, sugar, orange peel, salt, cinnamon, and bread cubes. In a separate smaller bowl, beat the eggs and orange juice. Toss these gently into the stuffing. Just before baking, stuff and truss a 10- to 14-pound turkey or place the stuffing in a buttered baking dish. Proceed either to roast the turkey or to bake the stuffing separately at 350°F for about 40 minutes.

Serves 6 to 8

# Thick Onion Soup

## INGREDIENTS

1/4 cup unsalted butter

4 large onions, thinly sliced

8 half-inch slices of extra sourdough bread

3 cups freshly grated Swiss Gruyère or Italian Parmesan cheese

5 to 6 cups beef broth

*Easy to assemble. Bake this cheesy soup an hour for a satisfying, simple meal.*

Melt the butter in a large skillet, add the onions, and cook them covered, over low heat for about 40 minutes or until they turn a dark, golden brown. Arrange all 8 slices of bread in a single layer on the bottom of a well-buttered casserole. Spread the onions on top and sprinkle the cheese evenly over the onions. Pour beef broth over all the ingredients and continue pouring until it reaches to within 1 inch of the top of the casserole. Bake the soup at 325°F for 40 to 60 minutes, making sure that the center is piping hot, before removing it from the oven. Serve the soup in the casserole directly from the oven.

# Black Bread Soup

## INGREDIENTS

6 slices dark rye
bread

1-1/4 cups milk

3 tablespoons
unsalted butter

2 onions, finely
chopped

6 cups beef broth

2/3 cup sour cream

1/3 cup heavy
cream

1/4 teaspoon
crushed anise seed

Salt and pepper
to taste

1 cup freshly grated
Cantal or Gruyère
cheese

*A hearty soup flavored and thickened with slices of
pungent rye.*

Soak the rye slices in milk while preparing the onions. In a
heavy-bottomed skillet, melt the butter over medium-low
heat and sauté the onions for about 20 minutes, or until
they turn golden. In a large saucepan or Dutch oven, bring
the beef broth to a boil. Add the bread and milk mixture
and simmer for 20 minutes. Carefully stir in the onions,
sour cream, heavy cream, anise seed, and salt and pepper.
Heat the soup but do not boil it or the creams may separate.
Serve the soup piping hot and topped with grated cheese.

# Bread and Cheese Pudding "Soufflé"

## INGREDIENTS

1 pound hot pork or Italian sausage (*optional*)

1/4 cup unsalted butter, melted

10 to 12 slices egg bread

1-1/2 pounds Monterey Jack cheese, grated or sliced thinly

4 eggs, at room temperature

2 cups milk

1 can (4 ounces) chopped green chiles

Dash of Worcestershire sauce

Dash of cumin

1/2 teaspoon salt

1/8 teaspoon pepper

1/2 pound sharp yellow Cheddar cheese, grated

Hot paprika

*The process of this and the following pudding soufflé, preferably made the night before so that their flavors mellow and blend together, translates simple ingredients into truly remarkable dishes.*

In a heavy-bottomed skillet, thoroughly cook the sausage, if you are using it, drain it, chop it, and set it aside. Melt the butter and pour it into the bottom of an 8-by-12½-by-2-inch baking dish. Fill the dish with layers of bread and Jack cheese. Blend the eggs, milk, chiles, Worcestershire sauce, cumin, salt, and pepper together, add the sausage, and pour this mixture over the bread and cheese. Cover the dish and let it stand overnight or for at least 4 hours.

Before baking, sprinkle the top with grated Cheddar cheese and, finally, with hot paprika. Bake the "soufflé" at 325°F for 1 hour or until the ingredients are set and the top is crusty and golden.

# Bread and Wine "Soufflé"

## INGREDIENTS

1/4 cup unsalted
   butter, melted

1 clove garlic,
   minced

8 to 10 slices stale
   baguette or sweet
   French bread

1/2 pound Swiss
   cheese, grated

1 cup dry white
   wine or vermouth

3 eggs, at room
   temperature,
   lightly beaten

1/2 teaspoon salt

1 teaspoon
   Worcestershire
   sauce

1 teaspoon Dijon
   mustard

1/2 teaspoon
   paprika

1/4 teaspoon
   pepper

1 pound tiny bay
   shrimp

Spread the butter and minced garlic on the bottom of a large casserole. Cover these with slices of baguette placed snugly together. Combine the cheese, wine, eggs, salt, Worcestershire sauce, mustard, paprika, pepper, and shrimp and pour the mixture over the baguette slices. Cover the dish and refrigerate it overnight or for at least 4 hours. Bake the "soufflé" for 30 minutes, uncovered, at 325°F, or until the ingredients are set and the top is golden.

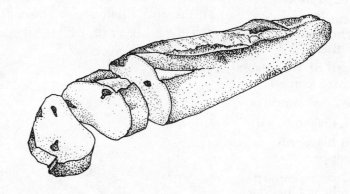

# Bread Pudding with Ham & Cheese & Spinach

## INGREDIENTS

- 1 bunch fresh spinach (or one 12-ounce package frozen chopped spinach)
- 1/2 pound ham
- 3 cups milk
- 1/2 pound sharp Cheddar cheese
- 3 jumbo or extra large eggs, at room temperature
- 1/4 to 1/2 teaspoon cayenne pepper
- 1/2 tablespoon Dijon mustard
- 12 1-to-1-1/2-inch slices egg bread
- 6 ounces unsalted butter, softened

*Sadly, bread puddings of late seem to be out of favor. Invite them back with the following refreshing versions. This recipe was developed by Curds & Whey, a wonderful wine and cheese shop in Oakland, California.*

To prepare the fresh spinach, wash it very well, tie the leaves in a bunch, and cut off the stems. Plunge the leaves into rapidly boiling water and cook them for one minute. Cool the spinach in cold water, then shake out the excess water. Wrap it in towels and gently squeeze until it is dry. Chop the spinach and set it aside. For frozen spinach, thaw it, squeeze it, and dry it in a towel.

To prepare the ham, chop it very fine either by hand or in a food processor. (If the chunks are too coarse, the pudding tends to fall apart when it is sliced.)

To prepare the custard cheese sauce, first scald the milk over medium heat. Meanwhile, grate the cheese. When the milk is scalded, add the cheese and stir the mixture until the cheese melts. Remove the pan from the heat. Whisk the eggs, cayenne pepper, and mustard until they are just mixed. Stir the egg mixture into the warm milk and cheese.

To prepare the bread, cut off the crusts and cut it into ¼-inch slices. Butter the slices.

Butter or oil a 4-by-4-by-12-inch pan (a ceramic terrine is perfect). Starting and ending with bread, layer the bread and the ham alternately, putting a single layer of spinach in the center. Pour the custard cheese sauce over the top. If it does not all fit, reserve the remainder until the pudding is ready to go into the oven. By then the bread will have absorbed enough sauce to make room, and the rest may be poured over the top.

If possible, let the pudding soak, either all day or overnight, in the refrigerator. In the evening or on the following day, put it in a pan of warm water (a *bain marie*) and place the pan in a cold oven. Turn the oven to 350°F and bake the pudding for approximately 1 hour and 15 minutes. If you do not have that much time, let the pudding soak for 1 hour at room temperature and bake it in a pan of warm water in a 350°F oven for approximately 1 hour.

## Variations

The pudding is also good with a part dark rye or all whole-wheat bread.

Cooked sausage, fried bacon, or cooked chicken or turkey may be substituted for the ham.

Parsley, chard, broccoli, or any other green vegetable may be substituted for the spinach.

---

Serves 10 to 12

# Bread Pudding with Rhubarb

## INGREDIENTS

**4 cups fresh rhubarb, leaves discarded, cut into 1-inch cubes**

**2/3 cup sugar**

**1/2 pound French bread, cut into 1-inch cubes**

**3 large eggs, at room temperature**

**2 cups half and half**

**1 cup milk**

**Freshly grated nutmeg**

**1 tablespoon dark brown sugar**

**1 teaspoon cinnamon**

**3 tablespoons unsalted butter**

Combine the rhubarb and ⅔ cup sugar in a saucepan. Cook, stirring occasionally, over medium-low heat for about 15 minutes or until the rhubarb starts to break down in texture. Remove the pan from the heat. Stir in the bread cubes and eggs. Scald the half and half, milk, and nutmeg and pour this over the rhubarb mixture. Pour the pudding into a well-buttered, 2-quart baking dish. Sprinkle it lightly and evenly with brown sugar and cinnamon and dot it with butter.

Place the pudding in a *bain marie* and bake it at 350°F for 30 to 40 minutes, or until the rhubarb is done and a knife inserted into the center of the pudding comes out clean.

# Bread Pudding with Cranberries

## INGREDIENTS

**1/2 cup sugar**

**3 eggs, at room temperature**

**2 egg yolks, at room temperature**

**2 cups milk**

**1 cup heavy cream**

**1 tablespoon grated orange rind**

**6 slices buttered egg bread**

**2 cups fresh cranberries**

**2/3 cup sugar**

**2 tablespoons water**

In a large bowl beat the sugar, whole eggs, and egg yolks well. Scald the milk, cream, and orange rind. Stir a small amount of the milk mixture into the egg mixture, mix well and pour in the remainder. Line a well-buttered, 2-quart or 7-by-11-inch baking dish with a single layer of bread slices, buttered-side up. Pour the custard over the bread.

Place the baking dish in a *bain marie* and bake the pudding at 375°F for 25 minutes or until it is *almost* done.

Meanwhile, prepare the cranberries. Combine the cranberries, ⅔ cup sugar, and water in a heavy-bottomed saucepan. Cook them, stirring frequently, over medium-low heat until the berries pop. After the pudding has cooked for 25 minutes, spread the cranberry mixture evenly over the top of it. Continue baking the pudding for another 10 minutes.

# Bread Pudding with Pistachios

## INGREDIENTS

**1/2 cup skinned and chopped pistachios**

**4 slices bread, torn into cubes**

**1 cup milk**

**1/3 cup sugar**

**1 tablespoon kirsch**

**4 egg yolks, at room temperature**

**2 egg whites, at room temperature**

**Pinch of cream of tartar**

**Pinch of salt**

Spread the shelled nuts evenly on a cookie sheet and heat them for about 6 minutes in a 275°F oven; transfer the nuts to a towel and rub them gently, discarding the skins. Soak the bread cubes in milk for about 3 minutes. Add the sugar, kirsch, pistachios, and egg yolks and combine the mixture thoroughly. In a separate bowl, beat the egg whites with a pinch of cream of tartar and salt until they form stiff, but not dry, peaks. Gently fold this into the bread mixture. Pour the pudding into a generously buttered, 3-cup baking dish and bake it at 400°F for 20 to 30 minutes, or until its top is golden and a knife inserted into the center comes out clean.

# Ice-Box Bread and Butter Pudding with Blueberries

## INGREDIENTS

**6 cups fresh blue-
berries (reserve 1/4
cup for garnishing)**

**1 cup sugar**

**1/2 cup water**

**1 stick cinnamon**

**Fresh lemon juice
to taste**

**Sugar to taste,
if needed**

**1/2 cup unsalted
butter, softened**

**12 to 14 slices bread
(try half white
and half oat or
other whole-grain
bread)**

**Heavy cream**

Combine the blueberries, sugar, water, and cinnamon in a large, heavy-bottomed saucepan. Place it over medium heat and simmer the berries, uncovered, until they have all popped and the mixture has thickened slightly. This will take about 10 minutes. Remove the pan from the heat and discard the cinnamon. Add the lemon juice and more sugar if necessary.

Butter both sides of all the bread slices and layer them snugly on the bottom of a mold that holds exactly 6 cups. Pour ¾ of the blueberry mixture over the bread. Cover the blueberries with a second layer of bread, then with the remaining blueberries, and then with a final layer of bread. (You may need a few more slices.)

Cover the mold with plastic wrap. Place a 1-pound weight (such as a can of food weighing 1 pound) on a plate and place the plate on top of the plastic. Refrigerate the pudding for 24 to 48 hours. Loosen the sides and unmold the pudding onto a serving platter. Garnish it with whole blueberries and whipped cream.

# Notes

1. Alice Waters, *Chez Panisse Menu Cookbook* (New York: Random House, 1982), 228.

2. Abby Mandel, "Breads from Home-ground Grains," *The Pleasures of Cooking*, March/April, 1983, 32.

3. People should question and investigate the purity of their salt. One source of information is the Grain and Salt Society (Happiness Press, P.O. Box DD, Magalia, California 95954). With a yearly membership you will receive pure imported salt as well as literature.

4. Ada Lou Roberts, *The New Book of Favorite Breads of Rose Lane Farm* (New York: Dover, 1960), 15.

5. Walter Banfield, *Manna*, 2d ed. (London: Maclaren, 1947), 202.

6. Heinrich Böll, *Group Portrait with Lady* (New York: McGraw-Hill, 1973), 17.

# Bibliography

Banfield, Walter T. *Manna*. 2d ed. London: Maclaren, 1947.

Beard, James. *Beard on Bread*. New York: Knopf, 1981.

Brown, Edward E. *Tassajara Bread Book*. Boulder, Colo.: Shambhala, 1970.

Casella, Dolores. *A World of Breads*. Port Washington, N.Y.: David White, 1966.

Clayton, Bernard, Jr. *The Complete Book of Breads*. New York: Simon and Schuster, 1973.

————. *The Breads of France*. Indianapolis and New York: Bobbs-Merrill, 1978.

David, Elizabeth. *English Bread & Yeast Cookery*. New York: Viking, 1980.

De Gouy, Louis P. *The Bread Tray*. New York: Dover, 1974.

Editors of Time-Life Books. *Breads*. Alexandria, Va.: Time-Life Books, 1981.

Jones, Judith, and Evan Jones. *The Book of Bread*. New York: Harper & Row, 1982.

Kamman, Madeleine. *When French Women Cook*. New York: Atheneum, 1982.

Katzen, Mollie. *The Enchanted Broccoli Forest*. Berkeley, Ca.: Ten Speed Press, 1982.

London, Mel. *Bread Winners*. Emmaus, Pa.: 1979.

Mandel, Abby. "Breads from Home-ground Grains," *The Pleasures of Cooking*, March/April, 1983, 32–38.

Roberts, Ada Lou. *The New Book of Favorite Breads from Rose Lane Farm*. New York: Dover, 1960.

Sales, Georgia MacLeod, and Grover Sales. *The Clay-Pot Cookbook*. New York: Atheneum, 1983.

Waters, Alice. *Chez Panisse Menu Cookbook*. New York: Random House, 1982.

# Index

# Baker's Notes

# Baker's Notes

# Baker's Notes

# Aris Cookbooks from Addison-Wesley

**Chef Wolfe's New American Turkey Cookery** by Ken Wolfe and Olga Bier. Master Chef Ken Wolfe and food columnist Olga Bier have compiled the ultimate guide to turkey cookery for the American kitchen. Carefully illustrated techniques, delicious recipes and basic culinary sense bring our all-American bird into the 21st century. 156 pages, paper $9.95 ISBN 0-201-11803-3

**Ginger East to West** by Bruce Cost. "This is one of the finest books on a single subject of food I have ever read. Ginger has become one of the most important flavors in America today; the recipes are fascinating."—Craig Claiborne. 192 pages, cloth $17.95 ISBN 0-201-17343-3; paper $10.95, ISBN 0-201-17344-1

**The Book of Garlic** by Lloyd J. Harris. The book that started America's love affair with garlic. It consolidates recipes, lore, history, medicinal concoctions and much more. "Admirably researched and well written."—Craig Claiborne in *The New York Times*. Third, revised edition: 286 pages, paper $11.95, ISBN 0-201-11687-1

**The International Squid Cookbook** by Isaac Cronin. A charming collection of recipes, curiosities and culinary information. "A culinary myopia for squid lovers."—*New York Magazine*. 96 pages, paper, $8.95, ISBN 0-201-19030-3

**California Seafood Cookbook** by Isaac Cronin, Jay Harlow and Paul Johnson. The definitive recipe and reference guide to fish and shellfish of the Pacific. It includes 150 recipes, magnificent fish illustrations, important information and more. "One of the best manuals I have ever read."—M. F. K. Fisher. 288 pages, paper $13.95, ISBN 0-201-11708-8

**The Feast of the Olive: Cooking with Olives and Olive Oil** by Maggie Blyth Klein. A complete recipe and reference guide to using fine olive oils and a variety of cured olives. 223 pages, cloth $16.95, ISBN 0-201-12226-X; paper $10.95, ISBN 0-201-12558-7

**The Art of Filo Cookbook** by Marti Sousanis. International entrées, appetizers and desserts wrapped in flaky pastry. 144 pages, paper $10.95, ISBN 0-201-10871-2

Available at your local bookstore. Or address orders or inquiries about these or other Addison-Wesley cookbooks to: Retail Sales Group, Addison-Wesley Publishing Company, Route 128, Reading, MA 01867. Order Department or Customer Service: 1-800-447-2226.